The Wall Street MBA

The Wall Street MBA

Your Personal Crash Course in Corporate Finance

Reuben Advani

McGraw-Hill

New York   Chicago   San Francisco   Lisbon   London
Madrid   Mexico City   Milan   New Delhi   San Juan
Seoul   Singapore   Sydney   Toronto

The *McGraw-Hill* Companies

1 2 3 4 5 6 7 8 9 0   DOC/DOC   0 9 8 7 6

ISBN 0-07-147008-5

This publication is designed to provide accurate and authoritative information in regard to the subject matter covered. It is sold with the understanding that neither the author nor the publisher is engaged in rendering legal, accounting, futures/securities trading, or other professional service. If legal advice or other expert assistance is required, the services of a competent professional person should be sought.
—*From a Declaration of Principles jointly adopted by a Committee of the American Bar Association and a Committee of Publishers*

McGraw-Hill books are available at special quantity discounts to use as premiums and sales promotions, or for use in corporate training programs. For more information, please write to the Director of Special Sales, Professional Publishing, McGraw-Hill, Two Penn Plaza, New York, NY 10121-2298. Or contact your local bookstore.

 This book is printed on recycled, acid-free paper containing a minimum of 50% recycled, de-inked fiber.

Library of Congress Cataloging-in-Publication Data

Advani, Reuben.

   The Wall Street MBA : your personal crash course in corporate finance / by Reuben Advani.

     p. cm.

   Includes index.

   ISBN 0-07-147008-5 (alk. paper)

1. Business enterprises—Finance.   2. Corporations—Finance.   3. Accounting.
4. Wall Street (New York, N.Y.)—Anecdotes.   I. Title.

   HG4026.A345 2006

   658.15—dc22   2006007022

To my dad, Indru Advani, the best friend I could ever have

Contents

Acknowledgments

A book like this cannot be written without the help of many people. I want to thank my mom, Dolly Advani, who has instilled in me the discipline and drive to take on any task, and my sister, Ramona Advani, who constantly offers her talents to those in need (which quite often is me). My deepest thanks goes to my talented team of managers at TeleStrat, Derek Minner and Jared Noordyk, who provided a tremendous amount of help on this book and who constantly deliver exceptional results. I want to thank Karen Usdan at McGraw-Hill for being so responsive and making this book a joy to complete. Every author should have such a talented editor. Also, Mary Glenn and Jane Palmieri at McGraw-Hill were instrumental in producing this book as efficiently as possible. I am truly grateful for their help. And of course, I owe a great deal of gratitude to Colin Kelly at McGraw-Hill, who helped turn my book idea into a reality.

Throughout my career, a number of individuals have offered me guidance, and I truly believe I would not be where I am today without their help. Robert Borghese and Fred Lipman have been tremendous mentors to me, and are always willing to offer valuable advice whenever needed. I truly appreciate their help. I want to thank Rakesh Jain and Sajjad Jaffer, my brothers in finance and always great sources of advice. Two individuals helped me find my way to Wall Street many years ago, Adam and Richard Pechter, and I owe a very heartfelt thanks to them for helping start my career.

Finally, I owe a special thanks to Heather Crake, who offered me tremendous support in every way possible throughout the process of writing this book. And assuredly, thanks is due to Montana, who, despite being only 5 pounds, kept me on my toes during this process by stealing pages and leaving paw prints on my exhibits. I also want to thank my friends Brian Buck and Mike Siegel, who helped keep me sane while I was putting the finishing touches on this book.

Reuben Advani

Introduction

The last several years have brought forth countless corporate scandals such as Enron, WorldCom, Parmalat, the collapse of high-flying stocks, and failed mergers of colossal proportions. And the cost of each has been ultimately borne by the investor and consumer public. The misguidance of investment analysts, bankers, accountants, and corporate managers has undermined our trust in these individuals and the institutions they serve. As a result, it is now imperative that each of us seek and comprehend the basics of corporate finance and corporate accounting.

But here is the bigger problem: finance and accounting are boring! I remember spending long hours in front of dry textbooks while trying to make sense of charts and graphs, let alone the esoteric vernacular. I have a confession to make: after two years at one of the top finance MBA programs, several years on Wall Street, and a teaching position at a respected university, I still can't tell you what most of these words and symbols mean. And this is coming from someone who has made a good living exploiting these concepts. A lesson that I did learn, however, is that certain MBA themes—if understood within the context of real-world business challenges—can be extremely useful.

So a few years ago, I thought to myself, why not put together a book that covers these concepts in a clear, succinct, user-friendly, and entertaining format? With this in mind, I have written this book, which is intended to offer a breakdown of the major concepts covered in a standard MBA finance and accounting program. My objective is to offer a user-friendly, interactive, and fun approach to facilitate understanding and learning. The book draws more on real-life examples and less on theory: it is part textbook, part storybook.

I have yet to find an accounting or finance course that is infused with any degree of passion. And likewise, I have yet to find a student of these studies to achieve any level of inspiration through them. But who says we can't try? If you can grasp the concepts covered in this book, you will be able to maneuver the world of corporate accounting and finance with a heightened sense of confidence. And hopefully, you will never again have to blindly accept the opinions of the so-called experts.

The Wall Street MBA

PART I

ACCOUNTING

CHAPTER 1

Accounting Basics

Q: What's the definition of an accountant?
A: *Someone who solves a problem you didn't know you had in a way you don't understand.*

Normally, the mere mention of accounting is enough to send most of us into deep REM sleep. And that is for good reason. Accounting is boring. But like a lot of other boring things in life, we still do it. Driving to work and getting our teeth cleaned are boring, but we still do them because we know each serves as a means to an end. Similarly, we learn accounting to assist us in tackling a number of business and personal challenges. A clear understanding of accounting, as well as the ability to apply the concepts, will lead to better decision making in our business activities. From picking stocks to calculating our own net worth, these concepts are useful. Plus, if we can apply them correctly to real-life vignettes and cases, they will be less boring, more fun, and easy to read and digest.

In this chapter, we will discuss the following:

- Double entry accounting
- Cash versus accrual accounting
- Creative accounting

- Generally accepted accounting principles (GAAP)
- Tax versus book accounting
- Introduction to financial statements

Double Entry Accounting

In accounting, a system called *double entry accounting* is used. This system is similar in concept to something you may have studied back in high school physics class. You might recall that for every action, there is an equal and opposite reaction. A similar principle applies in accounting. The principle is this: money is transferred from a source account to a destination account. In other words, money is neither gained nor lost; it is simply transferred. So when a transaction occurs on one side of the financial statements, there are one or more accompanying transactions that occur elsewhere in the financial statements.

Below are a few examples:

Example 1. A company purchases a product for later sale to its customers.
Result: The balance sheet would reflect a decrease in cash and an increase in inventory.

Example 2. A company sells products to its customers and receives payment by credit.
Result: The balance sheet would reflect an increase in accounts receivable and a decrease in inventory.

Example 3. A company borrows money.
Result: The balance sheet would reflect an increase in cash and an increase in debt.

Example 4. Finally, a company purchases a building with a combination of cash and a mortgage note.

Result: The balance sheet would reveal an increase under fixed assets (the purchase price of the building), a decrease of another asset, cash, and an increase on the liability side of the balance sheet, the mortgage note.

These concepts will become clear when the structure of the balance sheet is reviewed in more detail. For now, simply understand that financial transactions involve a dynamic interplay of accounts to create this balancing effect.

Cash versus Accrual Accounting

In financial reporting, there are two basic methodologies for reporting transactions: the cash basis and the accrual basis.

Cash Accounting

The *cash basis*, as the term implies, records transactions when cash changes hands. Suppose you walk into a local hardware store and purchase a hammer for $10 cash and you take immediate possession. Under the cash basis, the store owner would record this transaction as a $10 sale because the cash was paid and the item delivered—the transaction was completed.

Cash basis reporting is not generally accepted in business, but it is allowed for tax purposes in certain businesses that meet some or all of the following conditions (depending on the legal structure of the business):

- The business does not sell products, meaning it is service-based and therefore has no inventory.
- The business keeps records for cash receipts and payments.
- The business has less than $5 million a year in sales.

For the vast majority of businesses, however, the cash basis is not acceptable. Generally, only small businesses with service-based sales can use cash basis reporting. Most other businesses use accrual basis reporting, including all publicly traded companies.

Accrual Accounting

The *accrual basis of accounting* records transactions as they occur. The cash does not necessarily have to change hands, but rather a transaction must have occurred. Suppose that in a similar transaction you go to the hardware store, you purchase your hammer, and you take possession of your hammer. However, you pay $10 on credit. Nonetheless, based on accrual accounting, the transaction is still recorded as a sale by the store owner.

Accrual basis reporting seeks to capture the overall economic activity of the firm. This is because in finance and accounting, there is a fundamental notion that businesses are assessed not so much on what they have on hand, but rather on their expectations or potential. In the universe of financial reporting, what you see is not always what you get. Based on accrual accounting, the expectation is that the company will indeed receive those payments at some point in the future, although the reality may produce entirely different outcomes. More specifically, companies book sales when goods are shipped, services are rendered, or a long-term contract is signed.

At this point, it is critical to understand the differences between cash and accrual accounting. Suppose ABC Software announces a $500,000 licensing agreement. Under this agreement, ABC will receive payments of $100,000 each year for the next five years. Based on the accrual method, what would revenues reflect at the end of this year?

If you answered $500,000, you are absolutely correct, because under the accrual method, ABC would book the full amount—the contract is signed and the services, in theory, are rendered. This assumes that there is no follow-up servicing, so the software is delivered in its entirety. Under the cash method, how would this result differ?

If you answered ABC would book $100,000, you are correct once again, because ABC would record only what was collected. In sum, ABC collected $100,000, and that is what was recorded.

Creative Accounting

As you can well imagine, accrual accounting creates many opportunities for fraud and manipulation. The vague rules governing revenue recognition, along with numerous intangible items, create exciting yet often misleading opportunities for "creative accounting." The best example of this on an industrywide basis has to do with telecommunications companies using network swaps in the late 1990s to artificially inflate revenues. At the time, loose accounting standards in a nascent industry opened the door to deceptive methods of financial disclosure. The end result of this practice, sadly, was not unlike many of the cases we cover in this book: billions of dollars of hard-earned investor funds evaporated overnight.

For years, large telecom companies were plagued by steadily declining margins in wholesale network bandwidth. At the same, they faced mounting pressure to reveal strong earnings to Wall Street analysts. To alleviate these problems, telecom companies began the practice of swapping network bandwidth with other industry players while both parties booked the sale. This was done using what were called *indefeasible rights of use contracts* (IRUs), which are long-term contracts for use of bandwidth. Using these contracts, telecom companies would engage in a practice known as *round-tripping*, whereby two companies would simultaneously engage in a purchase and sale of an IRU contract with each party recognizing the revenue portion. Using this technique, one party would book the entire revenue amount resulting from the sale of the IRU contract. The same company would structure a reciprocal deal with its counterpart so that it was simultaneously purchasing a similar bandwith contract. In the end, no assets were transferred, but both parties booked a sale. The net effect of this transaction would be zero because they were effectively exchanging the same bandwidth. However, using accrual basis accounting, they were able to book this revenue.

How did they get away with this? When each side recorded the sale, it booked the full amount of the contract as per standards of accrual accounting. However, in the buyback, each side spread (amortized) the purchase price of buying access over the course of the deal, which at times meant 25 years or more. Alternatively, they might have booked the buyback as a capital expenditure, which would not affect the income statement and in turn have no effect on earnings. This method of accounting was advocated by Arthur Anderson's Professional Standards Group, which became widely regarded as the arbiter of accounting rules in the industry. As the pressure to meet Wall Street's earnings expectations increased, so did this practice, which was certain to boost earnings. In fact, one famous deal involved two industry leaders, Global Crossing and 360networks. Global Crossing hoped to exchange $150 million of its capacity for $200 million of 360networks' capacity. In the process, both sides would book revenue, although Global Crossing not as much. As such, 360networks agreed to purchase more at some future date to offset the current shortfall.

Such deals were commonplace and went unchecked for years. As share prices soared, the level of scrutiny on accounting procedures sank. But when such deals failed to compensate for earnings shortfalls, accounting regulators took a closer look at these practices and, more importantly, at the surrounding disclosures.

GAAP

The American Institute of Certified Public Accountants (AICPA) is a professional organization of practicing certified public accountants (CPAs). The recommendations of this organization have been vital to the development of the overall principles that we use in financial reporting and are known as *generally accepted accounting principles*, or GAAP. GAAP is for the most part considered to be based on the standards and interpretations of the Financial Accounting Standards Board, discussed below. When you read financial statements, assume that they are GAAP-based, unless otherwise stated.

If you have been following the news, you know that these methods are far from perfect. There are all types of loopholes that companies may capitalize on, and for that reason, we have seen numerous instances of accounting fraud over the last several years. GAAP is not without its shortcomings, but it is the overriding set of principles used when producing financial statements.

Who Does What?

A good deal of confusion arises over who is in charge of what when it comes to accounting and financial reporting. Essentially, the prime overseers of corporate accounting regulations and guidelines are the Financial Accounting Standards Board (FASB) and the Securities and Exchange Commission (SEC).

FASB.   The Financial Accounting Standards Board serves as an overseeing body whose mission is "to establish and improve standards of financial accounting and reporting for the guidance and education of the public, including issuers, auditors, and users of financial information." FASB is to accounting what the Supreme Court is to the law: the top governing body that issues standards and interpretations that form the basis of all GAAP legislation. Through a series of processes and subcommittees, FASB is granted the role of determining what is acceptable in financial reporting. FASB is not perfect, but it's the best that we've got.

The SEC.   After the stock market crash of 1929, a number of changes took place to ensure that such an event would never happen again. To this end, the Securities and Exchange Commission was formed as an independent regulatory agency of the U.S. government. The SEC now regulates all publicly traded companies by making sure that they:

- File annual audited financial statements with the SEC
- Follow accounting standards and practices as recommended by the SEC
- Identify accounting and reporting problems for FASB to address

International Accounting Standards

Businesses in the United States follow accounting rules prescribed by GAAP. Businesses in other countries, however, tend to use and apply their own countries' standards. This difference in accounting standards affects everything from the treatment of depreciation and amortization to the actual structure of the financial statements. Between some countries, such differences are minor. For example, differences between the U.S. and U.K. versions of GAAP are apparent in the treatment of asset acquisition and the tax treatment of extraordinary income items. But overall, the two formats are in relative conformity with one another. Larger differences emerge when comparing accounting standards in the United States with those of some Asian countries. And as cross-border mergers and strategic alliances become more common, such differences can create untold hassles in accounting for such deals. For example, a U.S.-based corporation that acquires an Indian-based counterpart will have to account for differences in taxes, intangible expense items, asset value techniques, etc. In large transactions, these differences can create millions of dollars' worth of accounting hassles.

There have been movements to create a worldwide standard of accounting, but as long as each country is confident that it is employing the best standards, such movements will probably continue with few results. But who knows? The best that we can do for now is to attempt to understand the basic tenets of accounting and buddy up to distinguished CPAs with years of international experience. And if you're having trouble with that, might I suggest *How to Win Friends and Influence People* by Dale Carnegie as some supplementary reading.

Tax versus Book Accounting

Very often, companies will create two sets of financial statements. One is reserved for tax reporting and the other for investor reporting. This enables the company to present its best performance numbers while minimizing its tax burden. In other words, this is the "have your cake and eat it too" option. Tax accounting is aimed at making sure that income and deductions reported on tax returns are in compliance with IRS rules and regulations. Book accounting, on the other hand, pertains to reporting on the company's financial statements and is usually in line with GAAP standards, but may not always be in line with tax standards.

Such reporting creates a fair amount of confusion for analysts and investors alike. In fact, companies that tend to maintain tight control over their financial statements and follow very loose reporting standards will tend to capitalize on the differences between tax and book accounting. Companies will often attempt the balancing act of trying to maximize returns for investors while trying to minimize their tax liabilities for tax purposes. So, in essence, it is acceptable for a company to use book accounting for investor purposes while using tax accounting for tax purposes. Companies that practice this approach must reconcile these differences based on an IRS tax schedule so that any changes or differences that exist between the two disclosures are documented.

Introduction to Financial Statements

Years ago, I was cramming for a high school English final. The exam was to be based on a number of books from the Victorian era, few of which had any relevance in my quest for a Firebird Trans Am. As I fully intended to devote more time to grooming my mullet and as little time as possible to studying Dickens, I devised a revolutionary study technique. In order to cover several books in a short time, I opted to read every third chapter of each book. In doing this, I could read three books in the time it would take most people to read one. Pretty clever, right? Armed with my new technique and a heck of a lot of confidence,

I poured through the classics in record time, and on exam day I pulled a solid A−. A few years later I tried this technique in college and failed miserably.

The moral to this story is simply this: you can read a few chapters of a book and get a feel for the plot, the characters, and central theme. But you will never truly understand a story until you have read all the chapters, word for word, and more importantly, understand how they relate to one another.

A similar principle holds true when it comes to financial statements. You should study the balance sheet, income statement, and cash flow statement for a company, but more than anything else, you should understand the links between these statements. Only then will you begin to understand the story behind the company. Unfortunately, due to the obvious time constraints of high-powered brokers and investors, many on Wall Street use my every third chapter methodology, which may explain why the world has lost confidence in Wall Street.

The next several chapters are devoted to specific financial statements: how to read, analyze, and project them. We will cover the balance sheet, the income statement, and the cash flow statement, seeking understanding of what each statement comprises, how each is used, and, most importantly, how the three statements relate to each other to provide a big-picture analysis. From there, we will learn the best ways to analyze these statements using trend and ratio analysis. Before we do that, however, take a look at how these statements are disclosed and what generally accompanies them.

Common Public Filings

Financial statements are filed periodically with the SEC by all public companies. Below is a summary guide to the more common filings:

- *10-K.* This covers the company's annual performance and is due 90 days after the end of the fiscal year. It contains:
  - Income statement
  - Balance sheet
  - Cash flow statement
  - Footnotes to the financial statements
  - Management discussion and analysis
  - Auditor's report
- *Annual report.* Essentially, this is a condensed version of the 10-K with more emphasis placed on marketing the company to investors through colorful charts and pictures.
- *Proxy statement.* This statement is offered around the time of the annual meeting and covers the following:
  - Management compensation
  - Management stock options
  - Related-party transactions
  - Auditor changes
- *10-Q.* The 10-Q is an unaudited statement of the company's quarterly performance, due 45 days after the quarter ends. It includes many performance reports, similar to those found in a 10-K.
- *Form 8-K.* This form is normally due 4 days after any material event (any major change in ownership or capital structure) and 5 days after an auditor change.
- *Form 144.* Form 144 is a registration document that discloses when insiders buy or sell stock.

Financial Statement Report

So what is generally found in the standard financial statement reports such as the 10-K and 10-Q? Aside from the balance sheet, income statement, and cash flow statement, companies will offer important accompanying disclosures. This documentation would include management's discussion and analysis, the management's report, the auditor's report, and the explanatory notes and supplementary information. These sections disclose any extraordinary items, any exceptional treatment of certain items, and generally any item that might merit further explanation. Below we detail each of these reports.

Management's Discussion and Analysis

Commonly referred to as the *MD&A report*, this company-generated analysis offers a strategic overview of the company's performance during the prior year, as well as anticipated changes in the coming year. Normally, this occupies a few pages at the beginning of every annual report or 10-K for publicly traded companies. The MD&A report is usually a worthwhile read, as it provides hints about the company's plans, goals, and expectations for the coming year.

Management's Report

Typically a supplement to the MD&A report, the management's report details the responsibilities of individual managers in preparing the financial reports. In the wake of the big accounting scandals such as Enron, WorldCom, and Parmalat, it is important to understand who is specifically responsible for the actual preparation of these financial statements.

The Auditor's Report

In the past, this report served as a relatively generic standard seal of approval issued by a company's auditors. However, in the aftermath of the big corporate accounting scandals and the adoption of the Sarbanes-Oxley Act, we have witnessed a new standard in corporate audits. Auditors will now explicitly disclose any red flags in their report.

Explanatory Notes and Supplementary Information

If there's one thing you take away from this section, it should be simply to read the footnotes. There's no possible way that I can stress enough the importance of these supplementary notes. To truly grasp the importance of this, read on.

Read the footnotes! Back in the 1950s, a gentleman by the name of John Rigas was working as a movie house usher in the small town of Coudersport in western Pennsylvania. If you have ever been to Coudersport, you know it is something right out of a Norman Rockwell painting. Behind the colorful five-and-dime store facades and below the cobblestone streets lie the remnants of a cable empire. At the time, Mr. Rigas, something of a visionary, read about the new technology of cable television and decided that the good people of Coudersport should have it. So with a $300 investment, he commenced building his empire. Within a decade, he had wired most of the town. Over the next four decades, he built a national empire that was now collectively managed by himself and his sons. By the late 1990s, Adelphia had become a Wall Street darling and the fifth largest cable provider in the United States. All this changed during one quarterly earnings conference call in 2002. This occurred after the Enron scandal surfaced and at a time when Wall Street analysts began asking more pressing questions. And on this particular call, one analyst asked a question about a footnote pertaining to company loans to the Rigas family. The footnote stated: "Certain subsidiaries of the company are co-borrowers with certain companies owned by the Rigas family." The question was followed by a vague response and the hasty conclusion of the call.

The stock price collapsed on the news, and over the next several days, a truly remarkable story unfolded, a story that documented instances of the Rigas family borrowing excessively from the Adelphia company bank account. This publicly traded company was essentially treated as the founders' own personal bank account. Among other things, they used funds from the company to pay for the construction of a golf course, a private jet, and even shares of Adelphia—not in the company name but the family name. That, along with clever accounting that included capitalizing millions of dollars in costs that should have been expensed, contributed to the eventual demise of the company. And what was ostensibly a conflict of interest was later determined by the courts to be a clear case of fraud.

The moral to this story is simply this: *read the footnotes*. Because within that tiny footnote was enough information to turn a multibillion dollar company into a penny stock. *Read the footnotes*.

Balance Sheet

A friend of mine used to live by the phrase *leverage your future*. As we were starting our careers in Manhattan, his extravagant lifestyle never ceased to amaze me. From his Park Avenue apartment to his vast collection of Hermés ties, he seemed to possess all the trappings of success. Yet he was always short on cash. In fact, each day he asked to borrow lunch money from me. I was comfortable with this until I realized that these were uncollateralized loans. So although he showed up to work with a new tie each day, I was subsidizing each with lunch credits. In fact, his "leverage the future" model was built on his friends' backs. Years later, I realized that numerous companies in corporate America employ this model . . . and my friend now runs such a company.

The balance sheet serves to outline this model by revealing what a company has, what a company owes, and what a company is worth (at least on paper). I like to think of the balance sheet as the doctor's report for the company, because it helps me determine if a company is in good financial health. It reveals if the company is strong, and if so, will it be around for a while, and if not, what are the sources of its weakness? Specifically, the balance sheet addresses issues of solvency, liquidity, and capital structure. The best way to remember the components of the balance sheet is with this equation:

$$\text{Assets} = \text{liabilities} + \text{shareholders' equity}$$

You might rearrange the equation to show the following:

$$\text{Assets} - \text{liabilities} = \text{shareholders' equity}$$

You can slice it and dice it any way you choose, but no matter what, this equation must hold true. If it does not, the balance sheet will not balance and therefore will not be a balance sheet. In this chapter, we will discuss the following:

- Assets
- Liabilities
- Owners' equity
- Sample balance sheet
- Balance sheet games

Assets

The balance sheet begins with the assets of the company. The assets describe resources of the firm that are expected to yield some future benefit for the company, such as an increase in cash inflows or a decrease in cash outflows. In other words, they represent what the company possesses. They do not always have to be tangible, but they should represent some value.

Current Assets

The asset section of the balance sheet begins with the assets that are considered to be most liquid, meaning they can be converted to cash, consumed, or sold within a relatively short period of time, usually one year. These are labeled as current assets. Some of the more common current assets include:

- Cash
- Marketable securities
- Accounts receivable
- Inventory

Cash.   The first of the current assets is the most liquid of all assets—cash. Most bankers would argue that cash is more liquid than water.

Marketable securities.   After cash, the company might list short-term investments, or what is more commonly referred to as *marketable securities*. These are generally liquid investments that the company could realistically sell within a short period of time.

Accounts receivable.   Accounts receivable, payments owed to the company, may also appear under current assets. Perhaps the company sold products to a customer on credit. The expected payment is then added to the accounts receivable listing on the balance sheet. Even though payment has yet to be collected, for purposes of financial reporting, it is considered an asset. The expectation is that the payment will be received sometime within the next year. In reality, however, this might not be the case. In certain instances, a company might list an allowance for uncollected receivables. This is merely an estimate of what might not be collected based on historic collection rates. A company might do this to more accurately depict the likelihood of collecting receivables or to create some flexibility in balance sheet adjustments through periodic estimate revisions.

Inventory.   In most nonservice-based businesses, the next listing would probably be inventory—what the company produced or purchased but has yet to sell.

Noncurrent Assets

Following current assets is noncurrent assets. The assumption with noncurrent assets is that these could be liquidated or consumed in the course of a year. Noncurrent assets are generally grouped into broad categories, which would include:

- Tangible fixed assets (usually listed as *property*, *plant*, and *equipment*, or *PP&E*)
- Intangible fixed assets (usually goodwill)

Tangible fixed assets.   Usually listed as PP&E, tangible fixed assets might include real estate, manufacturing equipment, furniture, computer hardware, delivery trucks, the corporate jet—anything and everything that constitutes the overall infrastructure of the company. Suppose you buy a dusty old dirt farm with your uncle and cousins. You would record the amount paid for that land on your balance sheet. Next, you purchase a shiny red Dodge Charger, weld the doors shut, and paint a flag on the roof. In this case, you would also list the price you paid for the car on your balance sheet. So your PP&E reflects the land and the car. Over time, your uncle starts to produce moonshine on the land, and your car has earned a reputation as the fastest in the county. Clearly, both have appreciated in value. However, for purposes of balance sheet reporting, both are still listed at historical cost. In a moment, you will see how most assets are assumed to lose value over time, even when the market might reveal something entirely different.

Intangible fixed assets.   Occasionally, an item will be listed as goodwill under noncurrent assets. Goodwill is a by-product from an acquisition and results from the difference between the price paid for an asset and what is considered its fair value. For example, when one company buys another, the purchase price is distributed among the separate units of the acquired business and based on the appraised value of the underlying assets. If the purchase price is higher than the value of the underlying assets, the excess is recorded as goodwill (which is usually the case). The idea behind this premium is that the acquirer believes the acquired firm will generate profits over time and the value of those future profits are recorded today as an asset.

Depreciation

A very important concept in finance and accounting concludes the asset section of the balance sheet—depreciation. This affects not only the balance sheet, but the income statement and cash flow statement as well. In theory, depreciation reflects the loss of value of a fixed asset over its expected life. As you can imagine, there is no scientific way to assess this. However, financial analysts and accountants try their best to estimate this by using a variety of schedules and tables. On the balance sheet, the depreciation listed is accumulated over the lifetime of the asset. To better understand depreciation, consider the following example.

If you have ever purchased a car, you know that the minute you drive that car off the lot, its value decreases. This happens because there is a certain amount of depreciation associated with it. Suppose you buy that shiny Dodge Charger mentioned earlier. You spend $10,000 on it. The expected life of this car is 10 years. If this car depreciates on a straight-line basis, meaning it loses an equal portion of its value each year, it would lose $1,000 in value after one year.

On your balance sheet, you would record the following under fixed assets after one year:

Year 1 Fixed Assets

Property, Plant, and Equipment	$10,000
Accumulated Depreciation	$1,000
Property, Plant, and Equipment, net	$9,000

So the loss of $1,000 in value is listed next to accumulated depreciation and subtracted from property, plant, and equipment. How would your second year look?

At this point, you would add another year's worth of depreciation to accumulated depreciation, which would appear on your balance sheet in the following way:

Year 2 Fixed Assets

Property, Plant, and Equipment	$10,000
Accumulated Depreciation	$2,000
Property, Plant, and Equipment, net	$8,000

Accumulated depreciation is the total of each of the prior years' depreciation. This continues until the asset is fully depreciated.

Depreciation is often a breeding ground for manipulation. For the most part, there are at least five commonly accepted methods of calculating depreciation, although companies will often use their own interpretation of these methods or choose the one that best fits their objectives. For example, a company seeking to minimize its tax liability might use an accelerated depreciation schedule, meaning that a certain asset depreciates more in the early years and less in the later years. In some instances, a company might have more than one depreciation schedule pertaining to a particular asset.

Depreciation becomes particularly complicated in new asset categories. In such cases, companies will use their own discretion to determine how to depreciate a particular asset. The result can have a dramatic impact on the balance sheet; and as you will see later, it can have an even stronger impact on the income statement because depreciation for that particular year will affect the company's earnings and, in turn, the amount of taxes paid. Depreciation is an area that companies will very often seek to maximize for tax purposes but minimize for investor reporting purposes.

Liabilities

On the other side of the balance sheet, you will find liabilities. Liabilities, simply put, represent the debts of the company, or what the company owes. Like assets, liabilities begin with current liabilities or those that in theory come due within the course of a year.

Current Liabilities

Current liabilities might include any form of short-term debt, such as:

- Lines of credit (amount outstanding)
- Accounts payable
- Current debt
- Current portion of long-term debt

Lines of credit. This lists the amount drawn from any credit facilities. Similar to credit cards in personal finance, lines of credit enable companies to obtain short-term funding with few transaction costs. For this item, only the amount outstanding would appear on the balance sheet. For example, a company might have a $5 million credit line from which only $1 million has been borrowed. Only the $1 million would be reflected on the balance sheet, despite the fact that the line of credit is substantially larger. When it comes to lines of credit, size doesn't matter.

Accounts payable.   This refers to amounts owed by the company to vendors or suppliers. Perhaps the company purchased raw materials for manufacturing but has yet to pay for them. Again, the assumption is that the company will have to pay within one year.

Current debt.   This might include any type of short-term bond or note issued by the company.

Current portion of long-term debt.   Often, when a company issues long-term debt, the amount due in the current year would be listed here.

Noncurrent Liabilities

Below current liabilities are noncurrent liabilities. Noncurrent liabilities usually take the form of long-term debt—any debt that comes due after the course of one year. Certain debt instruments will pay down principal each year as seen under the current portion of long-term debt. As such, only the portion of debt that comes due after one year is listed under noncurrent liabilities.

Owners' Equity

Finally, there is owners' equity—or what is commonly referred to as *shareholders' equity*. Owners' equity represents the book value of the company, or its value on paper. This is not to be confused with the market value, which will be discussed later. It is the difference between assets and liabilities, or in other words, what is left after the company pays everything it owes with everything it owns. Owners' equity consists of two components: direct owners' equity and indirect owners' equity.

Direct Owners' Equity

Direct owners' equity represents funds that are invested directly into the company by the firm's shareholders. This might include a sole proprietor of a small business investing seed capital to start the business, or it might be the funds raised from the investment of thousands of investors in a public offering. Either way, the funds invested directly into the company represent direct owners' equity. In the case of the hardware store discussed earlier (we'll call it Cunningham Hardware), assume that it was started by one owner with an investment of $10,000. That $10,000 investment would be listed on the company balance sheet under direct owners' equity, or what is commonly referred to as *paid-in capital*. Suppose that after 10 years, the business has grown substantially. The hardware store has expanded into a national chain with stores in all 50 states. At this point, a need for significant capital has arisen, and so the owner decides to take the company public. In this initial public offering, $100 million is raised. These funds are also listed under direct owners' equity or paid-in capital as they represent funds invested directly into the company.

Indirect Owners' Equity

The other component of owners' equity is indirect owners' equity, commonly referred to as *retained earnings*. Retained earnings represent the buildup of equity through the generation of income. This tends to be a bit more complex than most balance sheet items, so brace yourself. Retained earnings are very often overlooked, and worse, often taken for granted. In fact, many smaller companies will simply plug in this number using mathematical deduction, which ignores any deceptive accounting or fraud.

Going back to Cunningham Hardware, suppose the company reports $20,000 in net income on its income statement this year, and suppose the company issues a dividend to shareholders, which in total amounts to $5,000. When the dividend payment is subtracted from net income, the remainder is $15,000. That $15,000 is recorded on the balance sheet as part of retained earnings. It is then added to the retained earnings account. So retained earnings represent the amount left after net income is calculated and dividends are paid out. The balance sheet shows the cumulative of this account, which changes each period. The amount calculated on the income statement, which will be discussed in the next chapter, is based on the performance for that particular year.

Sample Balance Sheet

Figure 2.1 presents a balance sheet for Cunningham Hardware. The company lists its assets on one side and its liabilities and owners' equity on the other side, a common format for a balance sheet. Sometimes, however, assets will be listed above liabilities and owners' equity.

The first items are the current assets of the company, beginning with $8,000 cash, which represents the total cash reserves of the company. Next is $10,000 in accounts receivable, representing the total of payments owed to the company. The company has sold $10,000 worth of merchandise but has yet to

Cunningham Hardware Co.

ASSETS		LIABILITIES	
Current Assets		**Current Liabilities**	
Cash	$ 8,000	Accounts Payable	$ 3,000
Accounts Receivable	$ 10,000	Accrued Expenses Payable	$ 5,000
Inventory	$ 14,000	Income Tax Payable	$ 1,000
Prepaid Expenses	$ 2,000	Total Current Liabilities	$ 9,000
Total Current Assets	$ 34,000		
Noncurrent Assets		**Noncurrent Liabilities**	
Fixed Assets	$ 45,000	Notes Payable	$19,000
Accumulated Depreciation	$(23,000)		
Total Noncurrent Assets	$ 22,000	Total Noncurrent Liabilities	$19,000
Total Assets	$ 56,000	**Shareholders' Equity**	
		Paid-In Capital	$ 8,000
		Retained Earnings	$20,000
		Total Shareholders' Equity	$28,000
		Total Liabilities & Shareholders' Equity	$56,000

Figure 2.1   Sample Balance Sheet

collect payment for it. The reality might be that the company will only collect a portion of this, which is very often the case. Nonetheless, the full amount outstanding is listed here as a current asset, though it is not entirely liquid. Again, in financial statements, what you see is not always what you get.

Next is inventory, which represents the value of what the company produced but has yet to sell. The company reveals $14,000 worth of inventory. Whether or not the company sells this is inconsequential. For the purposes of balance sheet reporting, it is listed as a current asset. And again, what you see is not always . . .

The final current asset is prepaid expenses. This represents expenses that were prepaid and designated for this account in the amount of $2,000. Perhaps this company signed a contract with a vendor that spans more than one year. In that case, the total amount to be paid is recorded to this prepaid expense account and expensed periodically. In total, Cunningham Hardware has current assets of $34,000.

Next are the noncurrent assets, beginning with fixed assets. Again, fixed assets are what are often referred to as *property, plant, and equipment*—the hard assets or the infrastructure of the company. The assumption here is that these assets would take a course of time greater than one year to liquidate. The total value of the fixed assets is $45,000, which is based on historical cost. When these assets were acquired, they were worth $45,000. Finally, the accumulated depreciation of $23,000 is subtracted from the fixed assets, and net noncurrent assets of $22,000 remain. The total value of current and noncurrent assets equals $56,000.

On the other side of the balance sheet are the current liabilities. The company has accounts payable of $3,000. These are accounts that it owes to any company that has allowed it to purchase items or pay for services on credit. Perhaps Cunningham purchased several cases of hammers to sell in the store. The amount that Cunningham purchased these items for totals $3,000, which is what it owes to its suppliers. It also has accrued expenses payable representing expenses that have been incurred but are not due yet. Accrued expenses are the opposite of prepaid expenses and are expected to be paid in the period that they have been incurred. Common accrued expenses include wages and interest. In total, Cunningham has accrued expenses in the amount of $5,000. Finally, it has an income tax payable in the amount of $1,000, which represents the portion due to the government but not yet paid. Companies make tax payments based on estimated income. This account helps reconcile the differences between estimates and what is owed. In total, the company has current liabilities of $9,000.

Next on the liabilities side of the balance sheet are noncurrent liabilities. Again, the assumption here is that these noncurrent liabilities come due in a course of time greater than one year. The first and only item is notes payable. In this case, there is a note payable in the amount of $19,000. So the total of noncurrent liabilities is $19,000.

Last but not least is shareholders' equity or owners' equity. Remember, owners' equity usually consists of direct and indirect owners' equity. In most cases, direct owners' equity is listed as paid-in capital, which here totals $8,000. This represents the amount that the owner or shareholders of the company have invested into the company. Indirect owners' equity is listed as retained earnings, which in this case is $20,000. These retained earnings are generated through the accumulation of income less dividends over time. Each year, after net income is recorded and any dividends are subtracted out, what remains is retained earnings.

So total shareholders' equity is $28,000. Add this to current and noncurrent liabilities to come up with total liabilities and shareholders' equity of $56,000, which is a number that, not coincidentally, is equal to the total assets. The balance sheet balances and therefore is a proper balance sheet.

Balance Sheet Games

One of my fondest childhood memories was exploring my dad's great big Craftsman toolbox. In it, he reserved the cavernous bottom compartment for the tools that he owned, while on the top tray lay the tools that were borrowed from friends. So, in a way, his toolbox functioned much like a balance sheet. And if there were any tools he did not want me to find, well, those were usually hidden somewhere else in the garage—much like a balance sheet.

The balance sheet, in many instances, creates a great hiding spot for corporate managers. Nowadays, the use of this statement for such purposes is becoming increasingly complex. It is easy to understate a few billion dollars in liabilities or to overstate a few billion dollars in assets on the balance sheet. Before we get to the how, we should consider the why. As discussed earlier, the balance sheet serves as the doctor's report for the company. In other words, it reveals the company's state of financial health. This is important to investors, analysts, creditors, and credit rating agencies. For this reason, corporate managers will go to great lengths to reveal a clean bill of health that will often involve some clever scheme. Manipulation of this statement can occur in the following ways:

- Improperly recording the value of assets or liabilities
- Removing liabilities from the balance sheet entirely

Improper Valuation

As just shown, most asset values on the balance sheet are recorded at historical cost. However, new standards have evolved whereby certain items may be adjusted to current market price. Items such as marketable securities are relatively volatile while being fairly liquid, and as such, accounting standards necessitate that they be reflected at their fair market value. Other less volatile assets may be adjusted downward yet not upward. As a result, financial managers are often given the freedom to interpret these values.

As pressure to meet certain requirements for funding becomes greater, financial managers must ensure that their financial ratios fall in line with what is expected. For example, most commercial lenders require that a company achieve a certain debt-to-equity ratio, as well as current ratio, the ratio that measures current assets to current liabilities (see the "Ratio Analysis" section in Chapter 6 for more information). So when a company's current ratio falls below a certain required level, a financial manager may choose to overvalue specific current assets such as marketable securities. How and when those securities are valued will impact the end result, and in turn, the current ratio. The standards are loose and the enforcement of these standards even looser.

Off-Balance Sheet Items

If a company is seeking to maintain a solid debt-to-equity ratio, then it may simply remove certain liabilities from its balance sheet. How is this possible, you ask? With a wonderful invention called the *off-balance sheet transaction*. By meeting certain ownership stipulations, some balance sheet items can be transferred from the parent company's balance sheet to that of an affiliate company. It's that simple.

Most off-balance sheet structures involve the use of special-purpose entities (SPEs). These are some of the many culprits behind several large accounting scandals in corporate America, including Enron and Cendant. An SPE is formed as a separate entity loosely affiliated with a parent company and is based on specific rules of ownership. The SPE is created by designating a specific entity to carry out an activity or series of transactions related to a defined purpose. It is formed through one of the following structures:

- Limited partnership
- Limited liability company
- Corporation
- Trust

A minimum investment is contributed by a third-party investor, representing a legal equity ownership interest in the SPE. In exchange for this investment, the third-party investor controls the SPE activities while assuming the risks and rewards of its ownership in the SPE assets. For the SPE to be an arm's-length entity (not consolidated into the sponsor's financial statement), the third-party investor must bear the risks of the investment as well. Through such a structure, any number of items can be moved off the company's balance sheet, something that was done quite liberally by Enron (see Chapter 5, "Fraud and Manipulation," for more information on Enron).

SPEs are not considered inherently problematic or deceptive. However, thanks in part to Enron and a number of other companies, they have come under a great deal of scrutiny due to their ability to disguise liabilities. The SPE, when structured and disclosed in a legitimate manner, can be quite effective. A company can use an SPE as a funding source to lower its cost of financing. By isolating assets such as receivables in an SPE, the SPE can use these as collateral on debt. An SPE can also create research-and-development joint ventures with other companies, avoiding significant liability on the holding company's balance sheet. Additionally, it can finance real estate through tax-beneficial transactions. In fact, the majority of large corporations use some form of off-balance sheet structure. An SPE can also provide a needed asset without the accompanying liability. For example, suppose Cunningham Hardware continues to receive shipments of inventory from overseas. This is problematic because these shipments will arrive throughout the year, irrespective of demand for the products. The store is simply too small to display all items, and likewise, the cost of renting a facility is expensive. So management decides to build a small warehouse. By doing this, Cunningham Hardware can hold the inventory and pull from it when demand increases.

To finance the construction, the store will need to borrow funds. This will involve a significant capital outlay, which will undoubtedly affect the balance sheet. At this crucial stage in its growth cycle, the store would rather not reflect excessive amounts of debt on the balance sheet, even if it is for good reason. Furthermore, Cunningham is considering a private placement or public equity offering, both ways of accessing capital, and as such would rather investors see the strongest balance sheet possible. The best option would be to create an SPE to build this new warehouse. In doing this, the warehouse (the asset), along with the debt to finance it (the liability), would be excluded from the store's balance sheet. Cunningham can now rent the space from the SPE for a nominal fee and have complete use of it, without any substantial impact on its financials. Most investors will recognize this, provided it is disclosed properly, and will probably take little issue with it. However, problems arise when this disclosure is omitted or obscured.

Wouldn't it be great if everything had an off-balance sheet counterpart? A poor grade in a course could be transferred to an "off-report card," or a poor round of golf could be ignored as an "off-score card" round. Not a bad way to go through life. Soon, those clever enough to use this tool would be able to reportedly excel at virtually everything life has to offer. This is the mindset that fueled some of the biggest corporate scandals in the early twenty-first century and subsequently raised questions about the use of off-balance sheet structures.

CHAPTER 3

Income Statement

During my Wall Street days, I worked with a guy who made self-aggrandizement a sport. While the rest of us were pulling all-nighters to update spreadsheet models, he devoted his time to creating a certain image for himself. He made sure each of his superiors had at least a once-a-day telling of his latest dirty joke, a recap of last night's game, and, of course, a brief update on the projects he was working on. What was most remarkable about his approach was not so much his ability to charm his bosses, but more importantly, his ability to selectively disclose information. Most of his project summaries revolved around assignments that were in progress, were on their way, or had been allotted time on his busy schedule. His self-initiated performance report was a paradigm of good PR. He would overemphasize positive developments and underemphasize negative ones. And ultimately, he was judged more on the potential of these projects to come to fruition than their actual completion. Needless to say, they often remained unfinished. Each year, however, he received the highest employee rating of any of my colleagues.

This approach to performance caught my attention on many levels. But most significantly, I saw how not only did this colleague of mine use this approach effectively, but most of corporate America did as well. In fact, most companies had an official format for this whereby they could highlight their most recent performance based on things that have yet to happen. Plus, they could highlight other items that seemed more relevant to their strategic objectives. This format has a name. It is called the *income statement.*

I like to think of the income statement as the report card for the company, because it is intended to help gauge the overall performance of the company. How did this company perform on an operating basis? What were its margins? Are sales increasing? Essentially, the income statement helps analysts and investors to determine if the company is optimizing its potential on a day-to-day basis—at least in theory. However, in the world of finance, it's the student and not the teacher issuing the grade. The underlying problem with this is that the disclosure requirements are vague and leave far too much to the discretion of the company management. Companies can highlight certain items with the hopes that Wall Street and the investor public will look more favorably upon the company based on this emphasis. Simply stated, the problems include the following:

• Revenues do not accurately reflect what the company has collected.
• Expenses do not accurately reflect the cash that was paid.

The income statement is not entirely useless. It does have its purpose in that it reports the overall performance of the company, though often this performance may not be actualized. For example, as you will see shortly, the sales of a company do not reflect the cash the company has received. This is the basis of accrual accounting, which was discussed earlier. The idea here is that a company's performance is based more on its expected payments versus its collected payments. At the same time, a company may also expense or deduct what has yet to be paid. Ultimately, the timing of payments is not overly important in determining a company's performance. In this chapter, we will discuss the following:

- Income statement components
- EBITDA, EBIT, EBT
- Revenue recognition
- Inventory and cost of goods sold
- Depreciation
- Earnings release

Income Statement Components

A good income statement reveals a company with earnings that are stable, predictable, and sustainable. Of course, these are relative measures, and so they must be compared with the overall industry measures. Some of these comparisons will be discussed later in Chapter 6. It is important to remember that the income statement reflects the financial standing of a company over a period of time. This differs from the balance sheet, which is a snapshot of the company at one particular time. If you recall, when the balance sheet was reviewed, assets, liabilities, and shareholders' equity were listed. The value of each of these items was based on the end of the period. The income statement, on the other hand, tracks changes occurring during the period. To analyze the income statement, examine its three basic subcomponents.

Revenue

Revenues are a reflection of market demand and represent payments recorded in exchange for goods and services. The term *revenue* is loosely synonymous with *sales*, so if it is listed as sales, understand that they are essentially the same thing. Sometimes revenue will be listed as *net sales* rather than sales, which represents sales adjusted for discounts and returns. Because most companies follow accrual accounting, revenues are rarely a reflection of cash payments.

Expenses and Costs

There is a distinction between *expenses* and *costs*, although the terms are often used interchangeably. Costs reflect what is paid to produce or acquire the goods and services. More specifically, they are the costs associated with each unit sold. So in a company that manufactures widgets, the cost of the raw materials involved in the manufacturing would be listed under cost of goods sold, or cost of sales. Expenses pertain to what is paid to run the company on a day-to-day basis. Items such as salaries, rent, utilities, legal, marketing, accounting, telecommunications, etc., would be included in expenses.

Income, Earnings, and Profit

Income, often referred to as *earnings* or *profit*, is what is left over after expenses and costs are subtracted from revenues. If expenses and costs exceed what is listed as revenue, then the income statement will show negative net income, or a net loss. Otherwise, income will be listed as *net income*.

Common Items on the Income Statement

Below are various items that frequently appear on income statements.

Sales or revenues.   This item represents proceeds, either cash or credit, received in exchange for products or services.

Cost of goods sold.   Also listed as *cost of sales*, these are costs that directly tie to production. However, this is only listed upon sale of the item. So when an item is sold, the cost to produce or acquire it is reported here.

Selling, general, and administrative (SG&A).   This covers most day-to-day operating expenses, such as those mentioned in the previous section. Sometimes these items are listed line by line; but more often than not, they are grouped into this broad category. This is done for simplicity's sake or to obscure specific items. For example, when salaries appear unusually high, they can raise an excessive amount of scrutiny from analysts and investors. Rather than face questions about their executive compensation, corporate managers tend to prefer obscuring this number in SG&A.

Depreciation.   Depreciation is a noncash expense based on the reduction in the fixed value of assets. You saw accumulated depreciation, the depreciation collected over time, on the balance sheet. On the income statement, you see just the depreciation for that particular year, which is treated as a noncash expense.

Interest.   This pertains to payments made to service debt.

Taxes.   This will vary depending on how the company treats taxes, and more specifically, whether or not the company defers taxes.

Net income.   This is the company's profit, or its bottom line, what is left over after all these expenses and costs are subtracted from revenue.

Cunningham Hardware Co.

INCOME STATEMENT

Sales	$100,000
Cost of Goods Sold	$ 60,000
Gross Profit	$ 40,000
Selling General & Admin.	$ 24,000
EBITDA*	$ 16,000
Depreciation	$ 4,800
EBIT†	$ 11,200
Interest Expense	$ 1,600
EBT‡	$ 9,600
Tax	$ 3,200
Net Income	$ 6,400

* Earnings before interest, taxes, depreciation, and amortization
†Earnings before interest and taxes
‡Earnings before taxes

Figure 3.1   Sample Income Statement

Example

Figure 3.1 shows the income statement for our favorite hardware store. Cunningham Hardware is a company not unlike many others, public or private. Its income statement follows a standard format, beginning with revenues and descending through the different levels of profitability.

As you can see in Figure 3.1, at the very top, sales are listed. In the most recent year, the company recorded $100,000 in sales. Next is cost of goods sold. This represents all the costs associated with that $100,000 in sales, which total $60,000. That $60,000 is subtracted from the $100,000 in sales; a gross profit of $40,000 is left.

Cunningham's selling, general, and administrative costs appear next. This item incorporates all the operating expenses of the company. In this case, as is the case with most companies, they are combined into one category, totaling $24,000. Corporate managers strongly support this item, as it enables them to obscure the specific breakdowns of their expenses—especially executive salaries!

Next, SG&A is subtracted from gross profit to calculate *EBITDA* (earnings before interest, taxes, depreciation, and amortization), which is $16,000. From there $4,800 in depreciation is subtracted out to arrive at *EBIT*—earnings before interest and taxes. Once the interest expense of $1,600 is subtracted, *EBT*, earnings before taxes, remains. Finally, taxes are subtracted out to arrive at a net income of $6,400.

EBITDA, EBIT, EBT

Banker-speak is riddled with those fabled terms *EBITDA* and *EBIT*. These numbers are useful for three reasons. One, they measure profitability at different levels. Two, they enable companies to highlight their strongest level of profitability. And three, they make bankers seem more sophisticated than they really are. As for the first reason, it is useful insofar as it enables one to draw consistent comparisons between one company and the next or between one company and a peer group. In doing so, one can account for differences that exist between companies. For example, Cunningham Hardware makes interest payments of $1,600. Its nearest competitor, by contrast, perhaps does not have any interest charges because it does not have any debt to repay. Perhaps this competitor is financed entirely through equity. Aside from this difference, assume that the two businesses are virtually identical. They have a similar customer base, similar products, and comparable revenues and expenses. If you were to compare the two companies on a net income basis, all other things being equal, you would see that the competitor might perform somewhat better because of the missing interest. However, this is misleading, as it does little to explain how the companies perform based on their ability to generate profits. Rather, it underscores a difference in their capital structures, which is another issue entirely. In order to draw a fair comparison, we look at these two companies and evaluate their profitability before interest is subtracted. To do this, we compare them based on earnings before interest and taxes basis—EBIT.

What happens if Cunningham Hardware has depreciation of $4,800 while its competitor has no depreciation because it has no fixed assets? If there are no fixed assets, there is no depreciation. Perhaps the competitor simply leases its property, plant, and equipment. If you were to compare the profitability of these two companies, all other things being equal, you would see that the competitor might perform somewhat better than Cunningham because of these depreciation expenses. These differences might be further skewed as a result of the leasing charges that the competitor assumes for its assets. Regardless, a fair comparison is difficult to make because of depreciation, and as such, it may be more useful to compare the profitability of the two companies on an earnings before interest, taxes, depreciation, and amortization basis—EBITDA. Amortization, like depreciation, involves the expense or payment of an obligation over an extended period of time. Rather than expensing the item at one time, it is distributed over a period of time in installments. This might be helpful when a company has assumed significant research-and-development costs for a product that has yet to be launched. By expensing these costs over time, the profits do not fall drastically in any one year.

To summarize, EBITDA, EBIT, and EBT are used to account for the differences in interest, taxes, depreciation, and amortization—all variables that can affect net income. In an effort to better analyze company profitability exclusive of these variables, several levels of profitability can be considered. As you will see later, such profitability measures are also useful in valuation.

Revenue Recognition

The income statement is becoming increasingly important in detecting accounting fraud due to issues pertaining to revenue recognition. Earlier, we discussed the differences between cash and accrual accounting. You saw that most companies report their financial performance on an accrual basis, which means that revenues may not reflect payments that were actually received. As such, many company managers have gone to great lengths to book anything and everything that remotely resembles revenues even when the probability of actually collecting is slim. For that reason, revenue recognition has become a major concern for the Financial Accounting Standards Board (FASB), the Securities and Exchange Commission (SEC), and the investor public.

In 1999, the SEC issued *Staff Accounting Bulletin 101* (SAB 101) to address the issue of when revenue is realized or realizable. The bulletin describes a basic framework for analyzing revenue recognition by focusing on four bedrock principles established in GAAP. Those principles state that revenue generally is realized or realizable and earned when all the following criteria are met:

1. Persuasive evidence of an arrangement exists.
2. Delivery has occurred or services have been rendered.
3. The seller's price to the buyer is fixed or determinable.
4. Collectibility is reasonably assured.

The general framework and foundation for SAB 101 could not be simpler—it is based on the commonsense notion that revenue on a sale should not be recognized until the seller has fulfilled its obligations to the buyer under the sale arrangement. For the most part, the terms outlined by the SEC seem relatively straightforward. However, the last point regarding collectibility has raised a number of issues, especially in the aftermath of some particularly noteworthy scandals.

Informix

One of the best examples of creative revenue recognition comes from a company called Informix. In the mid-1990s, Informix, a database software company, made an aggressive play to compete with its larger competitors, Oracle and IBM. Informix cooked up a number of dubious schemes to boost revenue that had little chance of ever being collected. Once it was discovered that Informix was involved in such practices, Informix shares fell from about $24 to around $5 in a matter of months. The former CEO was convicted on a number of counts of securities fraud, and Informix eventually settled a multitude of shareholder lawsuits that forced the company to take a $94 million charge on its income statement. Eventually, the company was restructured, with the majority of it sold to IBM.

What happened? Essentially, Informix management was exaggerating the numbers by booking revenues before end-user sales were completed and by structuring loose barter arrangements with customers. Informix, from time to time, would enter into licensing contracts with certain customers such as computer hardware manufacturers. The parties called such contracts *pools of funds*. Under this arrangement, the manufacturer would resell Informix's software to end users. Then the Informix customer would agree to make payments to Informix over time, in exchange for these resale rights. Informix entered into two pool-of-funds agreements in 1996. In both cases, the companies maintained the right to resell Informix's software for a period of time as well as the right to make payments under the contracts to Informix. One of the agreements required that the company pay Informix approximately $6.4 million, $3.2 million, and $3.2 million by three separate deadlines. The other obligated the company to pay Informix approximately $4.7 million, payable as the software was resold, but with the total balance due by late 1997.

Informix would also recognize revenue from a pool-of-funds contract at the time it entered into such a contract, provided payment was due within 12 months from the contract's signing. As a result, this benefited Informix's revenue numbers by allowing it to include these anticipated payments, even if they were not actually made by the customer until a subsequent reporting period.

In the mid-1990s, GAAP rules allowed for the recognition of anticipated payments only if certain strict requirements were met. These requirements were unique to the software industry and included:

- Informix had delivered the software to the customer.
- Informix had no continuing obligations under the contract.
- The customer's payment, as stipulated in the contract, was fixed, and collectibility of that payment was probable.

More specifically, it was alleged that Informix management would enter into side agreements with customers, allowing them to cancel and seek a refund for payments made to

Informix pursuant to these contracts. The side agreements rendered Informix's recognition of revenue from these contracts on financial statements improper and not in accordance with applicable accounting principles.

Suppose a company tells you that you can use its product for a few years and you do not have to pay until later. Furthermore, you can return it for a full refund at any time. What if it is a product that becomes outdated after a few years? What Informix did was allow some of its preferred customers the option to use its software for a specified period of time, at the end of which they were expected to make the payment for its use. However, if the customer team was disappointed with the product, it could simply return the product to Informix for a refund of the balance paid. Not a bad deal. Informix realized that it could book revenues very easily through this method. In turn, it could inflate its net income, which would, hopefully, serve to boost the stock price.

Inventory and Cost of Goods Sold

The assessment of inventory values is a concept that significantly impacts the income statement. Generally speaking, there are two common methods of accounting for inventory, FIFO and LIFO. FIFO stands for "first in, first out," and LIFO stands for "last in, first out." Under FIFO, product costs are charged out to cost of goods sold, in chronological order. Thus, when items are sold, the value that is disclosed under cost of goods sold is done so in order of its original purchase. A LIFO system, on the other hand, charges out product cost in reverse chronological order; so the last item purchased is the first listed under cost of goods sold.

Confused? Well you should be. This is a tricky concept. Perhaps the best way to understand it is to use an example. Suppose you acquire four units of a product, one at a time. The first time you purchase the merchandise, you pay $10. A couple of weeks later, you buy another unit, but the price has gone up, and so you now pay $12. A few more weeks later you acquire a third for $14. Finally, the following week, you pay $16 for the fourth. In total, you spend $52 to acquire these four units.

Next month, you decide to sell these units in your store. At the end of the quarter, you have only sold three of the four units. Under FIFO, you sell the first three that you purchase, the $10 unit, the $12 unit, and the $14 unit. That gives you a total of $36 to list under cost of goods sold on your income statement. On your balance sheet, the $16 unit, the last one you purchased, remains in inventory. Essentially, the first units you purchased are the first ones out the door. The advantages of FIFO include:

• Inventory costs are closer to replacement costs.
• Expense and sales numbers are better matched chronologically, which is helpful in gross margin analysis.

Now, the other method, LIFO, "last in, first out," selects the last item purchased and then works backward until the total costs for the units sold during the period are removed. Going back to the original example, you acquire four units of a product, one at a time. You pay $10, $12, $14, and $16, for a total of $52. At the end of the quarter, you have sold three of those four units. You have sold the $16 unit, the $14 unit, and the $12 unit, for a total of $42. The first unit that you purchased for $10 ends up in inventory. On your income statement, $42 is listed under cost of goods sold. Advantages of LIFO include:

• Taxable income will be lower during times of rising costs.
• Assigning the most recent costs of purchased products to cost of goods sold more accurately depicts the current replacement cost on the income statement.

Cunningham Hardware Co.

Inventory Transactions	FIFO	LIFO
Jan. 1, Buy inventory (100 screwdrivers @ $10)	$1,000	$1,000
Jan. 15, Buy inventory (100 screwdrivers @ $12)	$1,200	$1,200
Income Statement		
Sales (100 units @ $20)	$2,000	$2,000
Cost of goods sold	$1,000	$1,200
Pretax income	$1,000	$ 800
Taxes (40%)	$ 400	$ 320
Net income	$ 600	$ 480
Balance Sheet		
Inventory	$1,200	$1,000

Figure 3.2   FIFO versus LIFO

To best understand how these two methods can affect a company's financial report, take a look at the two methods in practice. Figure 3.2 shows two inventory purchases. On January 1, Cunningham Hardware purchased 100 screwdrivers for $10 each. On January 15, it purchased another 100 screwdrivers for $12 each. Whether Cunningham uses FIFO or LIFO, the result is identical for the purchases. Cunningham records $1,000 for the first purchase and $1,200 for the second. The differences arise when you look at the income statement.

Suppose the store sells 100 units at $20 a unit. Using FIFO, the store books $2,000 in sales, $20 multiplied by 100 units. Using LIFO, it books the same amount, as the techniques do not differ in terms of sales reporting. You begin to see differences when examining cost of goods sold. Under FIFO, $1,000 in cost of goods sold is noted because Cunningham is recording the first purchase of inventory—the first item purchased is the first one sold—first in, first out. Under LIFO, $1,200 is recorded under cost of goods sold because the $1,200 pertains to the second purchase, or the last purchase—last in, first out.

When looking at pretax income, subtract out cost of goods sold from sales, and a pretax income of $1,000 remains using FIFO. Compare this with pretax income under LIFO, which shows $800. Now, notice what is paid in taxes. Under FIFO, the store pays $400, assuming a tax rate of 40% on that pretax income of $1,000. Under LIFO, the store pays $320, which is 40% of the $800 booked in pretax income.

Finally, the net income under FIFO is $600, whereas under LIFO it is only $480. Using FIFO, the store pays more in taxes but at the same time records higher net income. Under LIFO, less is paid in taxes, but there is also lower net income.

As you can see, there is a trade-off that a financial manager faces in determining which method to use, the trade-off between lowering the tax burden and maximizing income. Imagine for a moment that this is a multimillion dollar company by adding six zeros to each of those numbers. The impact is staggering. We see tax differences of $80 million and income differences of $120 million. So this simple accounting technique can account for millions of dollars in tax savings or millions of dollars in net income.

Depreciation

Depreciation is treated like any other expense except that it involves no cash outlay. It is imputed, meaning that it is based on a specific portion assigned to a specific time period. As you saw on the balance sheet, it is listed in its accumulated form, whereas on the income statement, it is listed as an expense specific to that period. Depreciation is usually based on the useful life of an asset and therefore can be subjective. Often, companies deal with new classifications of assets, especially in areas such as technology, biotech, and pharmaceuticals. In the case of new asset classes, it is not entirely clear what the useful life should be. For that reason, determining depreciation schedules is sometimes left to the discretion of the company.

Like most intangible items, there are a number of problems associated with depreciation. When businesses use an accelerated schedule, they will deduct more depreciation in early years, meaning they will probably see much larger tax savings in the near term. However, they are also going to see lower net income, which can often be perceived as a negative from an investor's perspective. Furthermore, different depreciation schedules will frequently pertain to different asset classes. Any new asset class will have few parameters. And for that reason, financial managers may take great liberties in how they determine depreciation for it.

Earnings Release

Each quarter, Wall Street analysts and investors behave like eager little children on Christmas morning. This behavior results from anticipation for the quarterly earnings statement that is issued by most public companies and can bring forth all kinds of surprises. This is essentially a condensed form of the company's income statement and offers a report card of sorts for the company. The most important grade on this report card is the earnings per share number. It simply records the company's net income applicable to each share of common stock outstanding. This number is compared with what Wall Street analysts predicted, and a number that exceeds this prediction will usually trigger an increase in the company's stock price, while a number that falls short can mean a drop. Of course, like just about everything else in financial reporting, this number can be manipulated (see Chapter 5, "Fraud and Manipulation").

Earnings per share is a very important number in this process of examining overall company performance. It is important because it enables investors to gauge how much they earned on an investment—how much net income per share they earned. Earnings per share numbers are calculated by taking net income and dividing that by total shares of common stock outstanding.

For example, a company reports $2 million in net income. If the company has 500,000 shares of stock outstanding, what is its earnings per share number? It would be $4 ($2 million in earnings divided by 500,000 shares of stock). This is a number disclosed by all public companies and affects their market value. It tends to be one of the ways that investors assess the performance and, in turn, the value of a company.

In 1997, the Financial Accounting Standards Board instituted a rule requiring companies to report earnings per share in two ways, basic and diluted. Basic refers to net income less preferred dividends divided by the total shares outstanding. Diluted reports options, warrants, preferred stock, and convertible debt reflecting their impact if they were exercised, meaning converted to shares of common stock. The growth of stock options as a form of compensation reached unprecedented levels in the 1990s, and as such, concerns arose that if and when these instruments were exercised, they would dilute existing shareholders. For that reason, FASB instituted this rule stating that earnings must be reported on both a basic and a diluted basis because any increase in the number of shares outstanding will indeed impact the earnings attributed to each share.

CHAPTER 4

Cash Flow Statement

One of the proudest days of my life was the day I landed my first job. It was an unforgettable thrill compounded by the fact that at a relatively young age, I would soon assume a great deal of responsibility. I was in charge of a business unit for a high-growth company. In this capacity, I managed logistics, procurement, and customer relations. And at the end of the day, I often reviewed the accounts. This process taught me a great deal about generating income—and more specifically, cash. More than anything, I soon recognized the importance of generating cash flow. Payments were often made by credit or check, but ultimately the strength of the business was built around its ability to generate cash. And my keen ability to reconcile cash and credit receipts soon earned me a promotion to the drive-through along with unlimited French fry privileges.

The cash flow statement is what I like to think of as the company's checkbook. It shows how much cash the company generated during the prior period, which leads to how much cash the company has currently. The cash flow statement determines if a company builds cash based on its operating activities, investing activities, and financing activities. Essentially, it takes the accrual-based numbers from the balance sheet and income statement and works backward to reconcile the changes

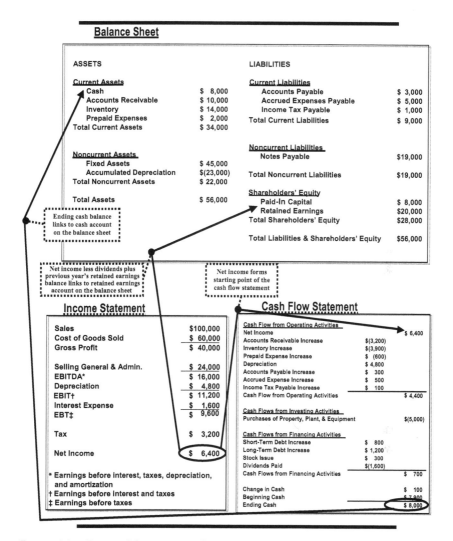

Figure 4.1   Financial Statements: Primary Links

in cash (see Figure 4.1). What is left over, usually listed at the end of the cash flow statement, is the change in cash for the period. That change is then added to the cash position on the balance sheet from the end of the last period, which in turn is added to the cash position at the end of the current period.

This represents the link between the cash flow statement and the balance sheet.

In this chapter, we will discuss the following:

- Cash flow
- Sample cash flow statement
- Why cash flows?
- Managing cash flows

Cash Flow

The cash flow statement is divided among operating activities, investing activities, and financing activities, each of which is detailed next.

Cash Flows from Operating Activities

Cash flow from operating activities is based on the transactions that normally affect the generation of operating income. This portion of the cash flow statement seeks to compute just the cash component of these items. In doing so, it examines the various changes in certain accounts to determine the amount of cash generated or lost.

Cash Inflows
- Sale of products or services
- Other extraordinary revenue

Cash Outflows
- Purchases of inventory
- Operating expenses
- Interest expenses

To build a cash flow statement, the preferred method is to begin with net income and then work backward to reconcile the changes in cash position.

Cash Flows from Investing Activities

Cash flows from investing activities involve transactions related to the purchase and sale of securities, land, buildings, equipment, and other assets not generally held for resale. Investing activities are not classified as operating activities because they have an indirect relationship to the central, ongoing operation of a business (usually the sale of goods or services).

Cash Inflows
- Sale of plant assets
- Sale of a business unit
- Sale of investment securities

Cash Outflows
- Purchase of plant assets
- Purchase of investment securities

Cash Flows from Financing Activities

Cash flows from financing activities deal with the flow of cash to or from the shareholders (equity financing and dividends) and creditors (debt financing). For example, in issuing new shares of stock, the company raises cash, which is in effect a cash inflow. Similarly, when a company issues debt, the cash brought in is treated as a cash inflow. When a company pays down debt or buys back shares of stock, these actions are treated as cash outflows. Finally, the payment of a dividend is treated as a cash outflow.

Cash Inflows
- Issuance of company stock
- Borrowing (bonds, notes, mortgages, etc.)

Cash Outflows
- Dividends to stockholders
- Repayment of principal amounts borrowed
- Repurchase of shares of stock

Sample Cash Flow Statement

Imagine that Cunningham Hardware is reporting strong profits each year while failing to achieve its expansion goals. Suppose the owner, Mr. C., is hoping to open new stores and perhaps even expand into new areas such as auto repair garages. In fact, his son's best friend has built quite a practice in this area repairing motorcycles. The possibility of expanding into this industry offers numerous advantages. One, adding a service business to a product-based business can usually help boost margins. Two, the strong relationships with hardware suppliers could lead to better purchasing power for automotive parts and tools. And three, the close ties to someone with experience in this business could offer trustworthy guidance in entering this new market.

So what is the problem? Although the company is generating decent profits, cash flows are weak. Ultimately, the decision to expand is a function of having sufficient liquidity, or more specifically, cash flow. Acquiring the building, inventory, employees, etc., will undoubtedly involve a fair amount of cash. Profits alone will not cover this, as profits do not necessarily imply cash. Within that profit number are payments not yet received; therefore a company can continue to generate strong profits while consistently falling short of cash. This cash shortage has slowed efforts to expand and is likely to create liquidity problems.

In an effort to better understand his lack of cash flow, Mr. C. consults with his business-savvy friend who owns the local burger and malt shop in town. After reviewing the financial statements, they draw a conclusion. The store is not generating enough cash to meet the goals of expansion. They quickly decide that some combination of the following would serve to increase cash flow:

• Increase collections.
• Sell fixed assets.
• Raise funds through a debt or equity offering.

Figure 4.2 presents the complete statement of cash flows for Cunningham Hardware (this is the same cash flow statement that appears in Figure 4.1). Each cash flow statement begins with net income, which is pulled directly from the income statement, as you can see in Figure 4.1. In this case, the store has net income of $6,400. From there, we work backward to reconcile the cash and noncash charges, which in turn will lead to a net change in cash for the year.

Cash Flows from Operating Activities

Receivables. The first thing the cash flow statement in Figure 4.2 shows is an increase in accounts receivable in the amount of $3,200. So on the cash flow statement, this increase must be subtracted. This is done because an increase in receivables between last year and this year indicates that the increase was booked as part of sales on the income statement, though the payments have not actually been collected. The sales line on the income statement reflects that increase, but the underlying cash is not there. In this

Cunningham Hardware Co.

CASH FLOW STATEMENT		
Cash Flow from Operating Activities		
Net Income		$ 6,400
Accounts Receivable Increase	$(3,200)	
Inventory Increase	$(3,900)	
Prepaid Expense Increase	$ (600)	
Depreciation	$ 4,800	
Accounts Payable Increase	$ 300	
Accrued Expense Increase	$ 500	
Income Tax Payable Increase	$ 100	
Cash Flow from Operating Activities		$ 4,400
Cash Flows from Investing Activities		
Purchases of Property, Plant, & Equipment		$(5,000)
Cash Flows from Financing Activities		
Short-Term Debt Increase	$ 800	
Long-Term Debt Increase	$ 1,200	
Stock Issue	$ 300	
Dividends Paid	$(1,600)	
Cash Flows from Financing Activities		$ 700
Change in Cash		$ 100
Beginning Cash		$ 7,900
Ending Cash		$ 8,000

Figure 4.2   Cash Flow Statement

case, the change is positive because the receivables went up. Because the receivables went up, that difference is subtracted since the cash is not in the company's hands. It is important to note that this is the change in receivables between last year and this year, not the actual amount that appears on this year's balance sheet. The number on the balance sheet at the end of this year is the total accounts receivable.

Inventory.   The next figure shows an increase in inventory. Inventory is not something that appears on the income statement. It is, nonetheless, a cash outflow because the company had to pay to acquire it. Inventory only becomes an income statement item when it is sold; and at that point it is listed under cost of goods sold. Until then, it remains listed as inventory on the balance sheet. Here, inventory went up by $3,900, which was a cash outflow, so it must be subtracted. Again, the purpose of the cash flow statement is to reflect changes in cash. Thus, the increase in inventory is subtracted out.

Prepaid expenses.   The company also reports an increase in prepaid expenses. These do not show up on the income statement but are still cash outflows that must be subtracted. On the cash flow statement, only the portion due in that particular period is expensed.

Depreciation.   The cash flow statement shows a depreciation charge of $4,800, which was also listed on the income statement. On the income statement, it was subtracted much like any other expense. However, on the cash flow statement, it is added back because it is a noncash expense. Although this was listed as a deduction on the income statement, that amount was not actually paid in cash. Again, the purpose of the cash flow statement is to see how much cash was generated or lost during the period, and so depreciation is added back onto the net income.

Accounts payable.   Next, the increase in accounts payable is reported. Accounts payable increased, and so the amount owed to vendors has gone up as well. Hence, that number must be added back. This is done because, although this amount is expensed on the income statement in some form, it has not actually been paid yet. So the cash position is effectively higher.

Other.   Accrued expenses went up, which are also added back much like accounts payable. Finally, there is an income tax payable increase, meaning the company has a payable due to the IRS. Again, this may have been expensed but has not actually been paid, and for that reason it must be added back. After summing these items, the total cash flow from operating activities equals $4,400. Note that net income is $6,400, but cash flows from operating activities are substantially less.

Cash Flow from Operating Activities

Net Income		$6,400
Accounts Receivable Increase	$(3,200)	
Inventory Increase	$(3,900)	
Prepaid Expense Increase	$ (600)	
Depreciation	$ 4,800	
Accounts Payable Increase	$ 300	
Accrued Expense Increase	$ 500	
Income Tax Payable Increase	$ 100	
Cash Flow from Operating Activities		$4,400

Cash Flows from Investing Activities

The next segment on the cash flow statement is cash flows from investing activities. In this case, the purchases of property, plant, and equipment amount to $5,000. Again, cash flows from investing activities pertain to one-time purchases or sales that do not show up on the income statement. The assumption is that these one-time transactions are not necessarily part of the day-to-day operating activities of the company, and for that reason, they remain off the income statement. Nonetheless, they are listed on the cash flow statement because they represent cash inflows or outflows.

Cash Flow from Investing Activities

Purchases of Property, Plant, & Equipment	$(5,000)

Cash Flows from Financing Activities

Finally, cash flows from financing activities are listed. Any increases or decreases in financing (debt, equity, dividends) appear in this section.

Debt.   This cash flow statement shows an increase in short-term debt. The company borrowed from a short-term debt vehicle, perhaps a line of credit, and in that process raised $800, representing a cash inflow. Next, it reports an increase in long-term debt of $1,200, meaning the company issued some form of long-term debt and in the process raised $1,200.

Equity.   The company also issued equity, meaning it sold shares of stock to raise $300.

Dividends.   Last, dividends paid to shareholders are reflected on the statement. That amount paid is listed here as a cash outflow because it did not show up on the income statement. Since it is still a cash outflow, it is subtracted. The total of these cash flows from financing activities reveals a cash increase of $700.

Cash Flow from Financing Activities

Short-Term Debt Increase	$ 800	
Long-Term Debt Increase	$ 1,200	
Stock Issue	$ 300	
Dividends Paid	$(1,600)	
Cash Flows from Financing Activities		$700

Ending Cash

The last step on the cash flow statement is to sum the three categories: cash flows from operating activities, cash flows from investing activities, and cash flows from financing activities. In doing so, a net increase in cash of $100 is calculated. During the period, cash has gone up only $100, despite the fact that income was reflected as $6,400.

Often, such dramatic differences between cash flows and income exist. This is related to the differences in accrual and cash accounting. The cash flow statement is designed to reconcile these differences. In this case, the increase in cash of $100 is applied to the cash position that the company started the year with, which is listed on the balance sheet as last year's cash balance. The beginning cash balance, listed in the statement as $7,900, is the same cash that the company had at the end of last year (the end of last year is the same as the beginning of this year—see Figure 4.1). The cash flow statement shows a cash gain of $100, which leads to an ending cash position of $8,000. That $8,000 is now transferred to the balance sheet, and in turn reflects the cash position for the end of this year—again, see Figure 4.1. This is the common link between the cash flow statement and the balance sheet. The cash flow statement shows how much cash was produced or lost during the period and is applied to the cash position from last year to get the current cash position.

A Quick Recap of Financial Statements

Now that each of the financial statements—the balance sheet, the income statement, and the cash flow statement—has been described, take time to note the essential elements of each. Figure 4.3 presents a summary.

Why Cash Flows?

At this point, you are probably convinced that the cash flow statement is an entirely confusing waste of time. Right? Not so fast. Cash flow statements have been required for all U.S.-based publicly traded companies since 1987 when FASB issued Statement No. 95. Prior to 1987, a less formal statement of general funds was used to summarize changes in balance sheet items, but unfortunately it lacked clear guidelines. As such,

Balance Sheet

•Assets = liabilities + owner's equity
•Balance sheet numbers reflect positions at one point in time
•Fixed assets are listed at original cost
•Liabilities and owners' equity provide sources of financing
•Current assets can be liquidated within one year
•Current liabilities must be paid within one year
•Retained earnings represent income left after dividends paid

Income Statement

•Income = revenues – expenses
•Income statements track changes over a period of time
•Income does not necessarily equate with cash
•Expenses may include noncash items
•Revenues may include payments not yet received
•Net income less dividends equals retained earnings

Cash Flow Statement

•Cash flows are based on operating, investing, financing activities
•Cash flows track changes over a period of time
•Cash flows reconcile differences between accrual and cash accounting
•Cash flows lead to the amount of cash generated or lost during a period

Figure 4.3   Financial Statements Summary

companies offered creative interpretations of such changes, rendering the statement all but useless. The new cash flow statement offered a standard format and a clear way to link the flows of cash to the ending cash balance. Over the last two decades, the need to understand a company's ability to generate cash has been on the rise. If a company continues to report strong profits while burning cash, that company will not be around for very long. This is something Wall Street loses sight of from time to time. Therefore, the cash flow statement is an important piece in the financial performance puzzle of a company.

The cash flow statement has been gaining in popularity given the proliferation of accounting fraud disguised through various income statement items. However, most Wall Street analysts and many investors tend to focus on the income statement at the end of the quarter, giving supreme weighting to profits. They often stress the fact that cash flows, by contrast, are generally erratic and fail to capture the true performance of the company. For example, a company can report positive cash flows one period, then negative cash flows the next. While the company might continue to grow by increasing sales and decreasing expenses, its cash flows could still be negative. In fact, the company might prove to be exceptionally profitable even though cash flows are increasingly negative. Cash flows, more than anything else, are dependent on the timing of payments and the reconciliation of noncash items.

Perhaps the best example of this is seen periodically in the automotive industry. Consider those great offers of zero percent down, zero percent financing. When automakers offer such compelling deals, sales may easily spike. Even though they are booking sales and, in turn increasing income, the cash is not there. It could take years before they start to collect. Because of accrual accounting, the income statement is rich with profits, while cash might be weak, with few payments coming in. However, this may be offset if the company has an independent financing arm that assumes the receivable while making the payment to the manufacturer.

Managing Cash Flows

Considerations

So what should a company focus on when trying to manage its cash flows (pay attention, because this is applicable in personal finance as well)? These are the main questions a financial manager must ask to effectively manage cash flows:

Sales. What are the company's sales for the period compared with the same period last year? Are there any dramatic changes?

Bank balance. How much cash is in the bank?

Receivables. How much outstanding is owed to the company by its customers?

Payables. How much does the company owe to its vendors and suppliers? How does this compare with receivables?

Capital expenditures. How much is the company spending on purchases of property, plant, and equipment? Are these purchases necessary?

Financing. Is the company paying down debt or buying back stock? If so, is there surplus cash to do this? Is the company paying a dividend? Is this something that has been done in the past? Does the company's performance support this?

Steps to Stronger Cash Flows

Companies face significant pressure to optimally manage their cash flows. In fact, I have yet to see a company that falls short in this area stay in business. No matter what the other financial statements say about a company, it needs cash to survive. Most respected companies tend to emphasize the following procedures in an effort to maximize cash flows:

Preparing detailed forecasts. Keeping track of detailed budgetary needs and expected revenues will help a company better manage its cash flows.

Setting up sufficient cash reserves. This goes without saying—keeping something in the bank will prevent a liquidity crunch during slower times.

Creating effective inventory management. Inventory is costly on many levels, and so keeping just enough to meet demand while avoiding surplus will contribute to stronger cash flows.

Leasing instead of purchase. Although this will increase operating expenses on the income statement, it will no doubt lower capital expenditures, which should benefit cash flow.

Accelerating receivables. The sooner those outstanding payments are collected, the stronger cash flows will be.

Decelerating payables. Hanging on to those payments due a bit longer can also help cash flows. But hanging on to them for an extended period of time can lead to questions about a company's creditworthiness.

How Much Cash?

A question that invariably arises is how much cash should a company have? The simple answer to this question is that it really depends on the type of business. On one hand, every business requires sufficient cash reserves to cover the day-to-day changes in the business. However, excess cash can mean lost opportunities. On the other hand, deficient cash can mean delinquent payments and lower credit ratings. So business managers often face this balancing act of maintaining just the right amount of cash.

In the late 1990s, Microsoft came under fire for building up billions of dollars in cash reserves. Critics argued that they were not using this cash to engender growth, namely through acquisitions and new businesses. However, Microsoft took a more conservative approach to cash management; and a few years later when technology companies were hit particularly hard by a weak economy, they were able to continue operating as before, with few dramatic cost-cutting initiatives.

Free Cash Flow

Free cash flow is a term that is often used in the world of investment banking. Investment bankers drop this phrase whenever possible, yet rarely take the time to explain it. In fact, as I discovered many years ago, there is no single definition for it. It can have a number of meanings, a few of which are listed below:

- Net income plus depreciation plus any other intangible expense during the period
- Cash flow from operations
- Cash flow from operations less some or all of the capital expenditures during the year
- Cash flow from operations plus interest and taxes

The bottom line here is to simply ask, how is free cash flow being defined? Frequently, financial analysts and investment bankers will choose the definition that best suits their objectives.

CHAPTER 5

Fraud and Manipulation

I n the late 1980s, a musical duo captivated the hearts of millions. With catchy beats, clever lyrics, and dazzling good looks, they kept young adults singing and dancing around the world. In addition to selling millions of albums, they won a Grammy. Yet every now and then, something just did not seem right. Suspicions arose that perhaps they were not actually singing during their concerts. But as they continued to sell albums, many fans cast aside their doubts. Eventually, the truth surfaced that not only were these performers lip-synching in their concerts, but they were lip-synching on their albums as well!

Nearly a decade later, corporate America was enjoying the fruits of the greatest bull market ever. Soaring earnings and skyrocketing stock prices became the norm for companies across industries. Although suspicions mounted that the numbers were not entirely accurate, few voiced any serious concerns. As long as the accountants, lawyers, and bankers were paid well, there was little cause for concern. Soon, however, irregularities surfaced, and certain creative accounting techniques that were employed across industries proved to be blatantly deceptive. Before long, investors and analysts came to realize that the numbers did not add up. We all know what happened next. Baby, don't forget the numbers.

History has taught us one thing—as long as companies are managed by human beings, fraud and manipulation will occur. However, as corporations become larger, so does the financial and social impact of such avarice. The boom years of the 1990s raised the need to exceed analysts' expectations and boost shareholder value to unprecedented levels. As such, corporate managers went to great lengths to deceive Wall Street, investors, and the government. Through elaborate schemes involving sales skimming, misappropriation of funds, improper revenue recognition, overstatement of assets, understatement of liabilities, etc., corporation managers created paper wealth of untold proportions. And as the web of deception unraveled, a costly price was borne by the stock market and the overall economy. If any good came of this, it is the painful reminder that each and every one of us should understand the basics of financial analysis, and more importantly, understand the ways to detect corporate fraud. In this chapter, we will discuss the following:

- Types of fraud
- Enron
- Profit smoothing
- Detecting fraud
- Pro forma financials

Types of Fraud

Most types of fraud can be assigned to one of six areas detailed below.

Money Laundering

Money laundering is essentially taking money from illegal sources and passing it through another business to make the money appear legitimate. For example, an organized crime syndicate involved in the drug trade might create a chain of dry cleaners to pass through money from drug sales in an effort to "wash" these funds. Generally speaking, money laundering tends to be a relatively low priority for the IRS. Could it be that they are more likely to collect taxes when the funds are "washed" and declared? For the FBI, on the other hand, it is a different story.

Sales Skimming

Sales skimming involves the deliberate omission of revenue to effectively lower taxable income. This could very well be the case with small businesses that only accept cash, as it would be difficult to track their sales receipts. It becomes a much larger issue when we are talking about Fortune 500 companies that use creative methods to defer revenue, or simply hide revenue, as was the case in many of the recent corporate fraud scandals.

Overstating Expenses

This type of fraud often takes on the form of running personal expenses through the business to lower taxable income. This is something that might occur in small, private companies, and generally it goes unnoticed on a small scale. It becomes a larger concern when looking at publicly traded companies, where a CEO might decide to expense his private art collection to the company.

Bribes and Payoffs

Often committed by large businesses seeking to fix prices or land contracts, this is the type of thing that occurs when a large company is seeking to capture a portion of some international market to secure a large account. Usually some type of bribe or payoff is offered to local government officials or business leaders to gain their approval. In my naïve younger days, while working as a financial advisor in Latin America, I found it a strange coincidence that when a lucrative privatization contract was awarded to a foreign bank, it seemed to coincide with the minister of commerce's purchase of a brand-new Hummer.

Shifting Sales and Expenses between Businesses and Operating Subsidiaries

Often, large corporations will shift expenses from a less profitable unit to a more profitable unit. This allows for a smoother distribution of profits, and in some cases, it can reduce the overall tax burden. For example, the more profitable unit may be facing an excessive tax bill. By adding expenses to its income statement, this burden may ease.

Phony Off-Balance Sheet Financing Schemes

Overall, off-balance sheet entities are not considered to be inherently deceptive. However, a combination of creative accounting and lax observance of ownership rules has created an opportunity to hide liabilities in them. As you saw in Chapter 2, a special-purpose entity is created to take on the debt of a parent company, and in doing so, the liability is essentially hidden. The perception is that the holding company has a much stronger balance sheet—something that analysts and investors prefer.

Enron

The granddaddy of all corporate fraud tales has to be that of Enron. Indeed, a number of other scandals rival it in size and scope, but the Enron story involved such elaborate schemes, crafted by some of the most respected leaders in corporate America, that we will probably be talking about it for decades to come. More significantly, we have only begun to scratch the surface in terms of what was occurring behind the scenes.

The Enron story began in the early 1990s when the company incurred large amounts of debt to help it evolve from a simple energy pipeline operator to a sophisticated energy trading house. Within a few years, the vast majority of its revenues were derived from the trading business. Soon after, the company was trading everything from telecom bandwidth to pollution emission credits. In fact, Enron officials boasted that they could trade anything including weather! Enron continued to receive accolades and acknowledgment for its innovative ideas, aggressive culture, and astronomical growth. In 2001, Enron was named the most innovative company in America by *Fortune* magazine—a well-deserved honor had it pertained to accounting practices.

The Enron story started to unravel when the company took large write-downs in its telecom and water businesses. In October 2001, Enron announced a restatement of earnings for the past five years, and between October 2001 and February 2002 Enron lost approximately $80 billion in market value. In fact, even while executives were selling some $1 billion worth of stock as the scandal unfolded, Enron officials were encouraging their employees to buy more stock.

What happened? Unfortunately, we may never know exactly what happened. Thousands of pages of documents were lost or shredded, and parties allegedly involved have offered conflicting accounts of what occurred. What we do know is detailed below.

Special-Purpose Entities

Some 3,000 special-purpose entities (SPEs) were created to hide billions of dollars of debt through skillfully devised off-balance sheet limited partnerships. They included names like Chewco Investments and Joint Energy Development Investments (JEDI). Any idea where these names came from? Enron's management and employees were so captivated by the *Star Wars* movies that they went so far as to disguise their capital base through character names from them (Enron headquarters was affectionately termed *The Death Star*). Enron funded the SPEs with its own stock, while the SPEs issued dividends on Enron's stock to create an artificial source of revenue. This system worked as long as stock prices increased.

Shifting Expenses

Enron hid expenses by shifting them from one SPE to another. This allowed the company to artificially inflate profits.

Revenue Manipulation

Enron would purchase oil and gas rights and record the value of reserves as revenues using mark-to-market accounting. This type of accounting involves adjusting items to their fair market value. However, in the case of Enron, the company used this as justification to value these reserves off the expected returns discounted to present value. Essentially, these revenues were grounded entirely in speculation.

Enron would also sell ownership of power projects to its SPEs, which would in turn sell contracts for that power back to Enron. Additionally, Enron would sell fiber-optic cable contracts to the SPEs and record earnings from the sale.

Price Fixing

Enron was involved in a major energy price-fixing scheme that led to energy shortages in California.

Why Did This Occur?

Two questions invariably follow a discussion on Enron—how did this occur, and why didn't someone say something sooner? The why tends to be simpler. When lawyers, bankers, and accountants are paid a lot of money, who stops to ask questions? Indeed, many company insiders and affiliates sensed that something was rotten in the state of Texas, but as long as times were good and people were paid well, few questions were asked.

So how did everyone fail to see this? This is a bit more complex. Take a look at the footnote below from page 38 of Enron's 2000 annual report:

> *Securitizations. From time to time, Enron sells interests in certain of its financial assets. Some of these sales are completed in securitizations, in which Enron concurrently enters into swaps associated with the underlying assets, which limit the risks assumed by the purchaser. Such swaps are adjusted to fair value using quoted market prices, if available, or estimated fair value based on management's best estimate of the present value of future cash flow. These swaps are included in Price Risk Management activities above as equity investments.*

Aside from revealing management's mastery of the written word, this passage reveals little more. In fact, rather than clarify an issue, it further complicates it. One, it fails to specify which assets were sold or when this occurred. Two, it offers little detail on the securitizations and even less on the swaps associated with them. Three, it gives virtually no indication of how these swaps are valued, being so bold as to state that it might be based on "management's best estimate." Such disclosures are prevalent throughout Enron's financial statements.

To further understand how most of Wall Street failed to uncover such egregious fraud, take a look at Enron's income statement from 2000, reproduced in Figure 5.1. Here you can see a company that reports over $100 billion in revenues with no more than four lines to outline what contributed to it. In fact, the financials for Cunningham Hardware are more comprehensive than this. So the combination of limited financial disclosure, vague footnotes, and a soaring stock price will serve to limit the number of questions about how a company does business—for some time, at least.

Profit Smoothing

Nowadays we hear a lot about *profit smoothing*. This is a broad term used to describe the practice of intentionally deflating or inflating profits depending on the objective. In fact, many publicly traded companies will engage in some form of profit smoothing for reasons ranging from beating analysts' expectations, to displaying steady growth, to reducing tax liabilities. Managers might do this by deferring revenues and expenses to subsequent periods. By waiting to book revenues or prepaying expected expenses, a company can limit its tax burden in the near term. Such tax savings can be of particular use to a cash-strapped company. A company seeking to boost earnings in an effort to appease Wall Street analysts and shareholders might record a pending sale in the current period. This practice is highly suspect and in most cases considered outright fraud; yet companies have been doing just this for years. When reviewing financial statements, it is

ENRON CORP. AND SUBSIDIARIES
CONSOLIDATED INCOME STATEMENT

(In millions, except per share amounts)	Year ended December 31,		
	2000	1999	1998
Revenues			
Natural gas and other products	$50,500	$19,536	$13,276
Electricity	33,823	15,238	13,939
Metals	9,234	-	-
Other	7,232	5,338	4,045
Total revenues	100,789	40,112	31,260
Costs and Expenses			
Cost of gas, electricity, metals and other products	94,517	34,761	26,381
Operating expenses	3,184	3,045	2,473
Depreciation, depletion and amortization	855	870	827
Taxes, other than income taxes	280	193	201
Impairment of long-lived assets	-	441	-
Total costs and expenses	98,836	39,310	29,882
Operating Income	1,953	802	1,378
Other Income and Deductions			
Equity in earnings of unconsolidated equity affiliates	87	309	97
Gains on sales of non-merchant assets	146	541	56
Gain on the isauance of stock by TNPC, Inc.	121	-	-
Interest income	212	162	88
Other income, net	(37)	181	(37)
Income Before Interest, Minority Interests and Income Taxes	2,482	1,995	1,582
Interest and related charges, net	838	656	550
Dividends on company-obligated preferred securities of subsidiaries	77	76	77
Minority interests	154	135	77
Income tax expense	434	104	175
Net income before cumulative effect of accounting changes	979	1,024	703
Cumulative effect of accounting changes, net of tax	-	(131)	-
Net Income	979	893	703
Preferred stock dividends	83	66	17
Earnings on Common Stock	$ 896	$ 827	$ 686
Earnings per Share of Common Stock			
Basic			
Before cumulative effect of accounting changes	$ 1.22	$ 1.36	$ 1.07
Cumulative effect of accounting changes	-	(0.19)	-
Basic earnings per share	$ 1.22	$ 1.17	$ 1.07
Diluted			
Before cumulative effect of accounting changes	$ 1.12	$ 1.27	$ 1.01
Cumulative effect of accounting changes	-	(0.17)	-
Diluted earnings per share	$ 1.12	$ 1.10	$ 1.01
Average Number of Common Shares Used in Computation			
Basic	736	705	642
Diluted	814	769	695

Figure 5.1   Enron's Income Statement

important to read the footnotes and understand exactly how revenues are treated, and more importantly, when they are recorded.

Detecting Fraud

So how do we spot these red flags? Among other things, it is absolutely imperative that we read the financial statements as well as the footnotes. In particular, we should be aware of certain items that can be a cause for concern. These include:

Stock option awards. Stock options, when exercised, can have a strong dilutive effect on existing shares. It is important to understand what this impact might be, and so the best recourse is to discuss this with company management or investor relations if it is not specifically outlined in the footnotes.

Pending lawsuits and investigations. Any type of adverse news can serve to undermine company valuation. Again, it is important to understand the potential outcome of these lawsuits and investigations.

Segment information. It is very important to understand the specific segments in which the company operates and how the company has performed within these segments. Segment laggards tend to bring the overall company performance down, and unfortunately, not all companies will disclose how they perform on a segment-by-segment basis.

Off-balance sheet entities. Anytime you see discussion related to more off-balance sheet entities or other special-purpose entities, it is important to ask how these were structured and for what purpose. Off-balance sheet entities can mean hidden liabilities.

Pro Forma Financials

The use of pro forma financials has raised a number of concerns recently. Pro forma financials are essentially adjusted financial statements. For our purposes, pro forma financials tend to fall into one of two broad categories:

- Adjusted earnings
- Projections

Over the last few years, companies have encountered a fair amount of scrutiny when it comes to pro formas. The simple reason has to do with the loose standards governing their preparation. The SEC recently released the following statement about this:

> . . . *we believe it is appropriate to sound a warning to public companies and other registrants who present to the public their earnings and results of operations on the basis of methodologies other than Generally Accepted Accounting Principles ("GAAP"). This presentation in an earnings release is often referred to as "pro forma" financial information.*

Pro forma financials are derived by selective editing of information, which can easily mislead investors. Through their use, a company can effortlessly present a deceptive view of operating performance. In fact, statements about a company's financial results that are true may still be misleading if they omit material information. From time to time, companies will use a pro forma disclosure to reflect a loss as if it were a profit. Consider the case of Amazon. In 2001, the company announced its first pro forma profit by excluding charges for stock compensation, restructuring charges, and amortization of goodwill. Simple exclusions provided a huge PR coup for the company. And the stock market loves good PR.

Adjusted Earnings

This is used to determine variations on earnings by omitting or including certain extraordinary items on the income statement. One-time charges and write-offs can easily be overlooked, thus turning a loss into a profit. Because there are no consistent standards or regulations for this, companies are able to use their own discretion in crafting informal disclosure and press releases to boost investor appeal. Reasons for this practice include:

- Providing a meaningful comparison to results for the same period of prior years
- Emphasizing the results of core operations
- Exceeding Wall Street analysts' expectations
- Impressing shareholders

The more frequent exclusions include:

- Restructuring charges
- Write-downs of assets
- Stock option expenses
- Write-offs of research and development costs
- Litigation costs
- Merger-related expenses

In the sample income statement shown in Figure 5.2, notice how any of the several extraordinary items can be excluded to create stronger earnings numbers.

Projections

Companies will often use pro formas to show the impact of a planned transaction or to spell out expected results. Such

Actual Numbers			Pro Forma		
Net Sales		$3,589,234	Net Sales		$3,589,234
Cost of Goods Sold		$1,567,321	Cost of Goods Sold		$1,567,321
Gross Profit		$2,021,913	Gross Profit		$2,021,913
SG&A		$ 890,487	SG&A		$ 890,487
Other Charges			EBITDA		$1,131,426
Amortization of Goodwill	$	23,965			
Impairment of Assets	$	14,864	Depreciation		$ 134,965
Associated Merger Charges	$	106			
Total Other Charges	$	38,935	EBIT		$ 996,461
Depreciation	$	134,965	Interest		$ 34,688
Interest	$	34,688	EBT		$ 961,773
Income Taxes	$	276,851			
Net Income	$	645,987	Other Charges		
			Amortization of Goodwill	$	23,965
			Impairment of Assets	$	14,864
			Associated Merger Charges	$	106
			Total Other Charges	$	38,935
			Income Taxes		$ 276,851
			Net Income		$ 645,987

Figure 5.2   Sample Pro Forma Income Statement

statements are useful provided they are detailed and understood to be based solely on estimates. For example, a company might use pro forma financials to illustrate the expected capital structure and performance of a company after a merger. The company would then issue a pro forma balance sheet, income statement, and cash flow statement. Such disclosure would be useful for planning purposes. A company might also detail the impact of a capital-raising transaction such as a stock or debt offering. In doing so, a pro forma balance sheet is revealed. Finally, for purposes of valuation, pro formas are a must. Future cash flows and multiples are usually based on some expected results, which necessitate the creation of pro formas.

How are projections formed? Unfortunately, there are no clear rules for developing financial projections. Yet many financial decisions are based on analysis stemming from projections.

Whether it is valuation or capital budgeting, a projection forms the most time-intensive component of the process.

Financial models are useful for the following:

- Building forecasts and budgets
- Assessing funding requirements
- Creating marketing or operational strategies
- Doing business planning
- Raising capital
- Conducting financial analysis
- Determining valuation

There are several ways to form projections, but the best ones tend to have a line-by-line justification for each assumption. Among the more common techniques are the following:

- Line-by-line forecasts for all components of the balance sheet, income statement, and cash flow statement
- Simple growth rate based on historic averages applied to the individual components of financials
- Economic growth rate applied to company performance

Of these, the first method is by far the most widely accepted, and when done correctly, the most credible. So what does it mean to build a credible forecasting model? For starters, the company has to reflect a current set of financials from which to build on. It can project out any number of years, provided it has sufficient information, but five years tends to be the standard in most industries. With the most recent balance sheet, income statement, and cash flow statement, a company can start to construct its projections. Usually, more emphasis is placed on income statement projections; yet more time is devoted to the sales aspect of them. If you have ever taken an introductory economics course, you might recall that sales are a function of the following:

$$\text{Price } (P) \times \text{quantity } (Q) = \text{total sales}$$

Therefore, assumptions will have to be made for both P and Q in each projected period. The company would have to consider the price of each product and the expected quantities to be sold, year after year. As you can imagine, in a large corporation, this can prove to be a daunting task.

So come take a stroll with me down memory lane as I seek to reconstruct the steps in creating a forecasting model. Feel free to read out loud to your friends and family as they too can share in the joys of building a financial model!

Step One.   Choose the right mood music—it's always a good idea to set the mood when preparing a good financial model. Given that you will probably be spending the next several dozen or so hours staring at a computer monitor, this will soothe the pain. My favorite selections in the past included *Pressure* by Billy Joel and *Please Shoot Me*, a little something I put together and enjoyed serenading my coworkers with during my Wall Street days. Unfortunately, the lyrics are not provided in this book, so you will have to make up your own, which should be no trouble.

Step Two.   Review the current financials along with those of the prior three years. Pay close attention to any trends, any extraordinary items, and any changes in accounting policies.

Step Three.   Begin to forecast your income statement. Take a look at current sales and determine the best method for doing this. In the most detailed models, you would form volume forecasts for each product. You would multiply these volume numbers by pricing estimates for each product.

Step Four.   Measure all variable costs, namely your cost of goods sold. You can model these individually based on estimated price forecasts or based on a percentage of sales.

Step Five.   Estimate operating expenses for each of the next five years. This can be fairly simple if you expect operating expenses to remain relatively flat. In particular, you must give thought to number of employees, salaries, marketing, legal, utilities, etc. If you are projecting substantial sales growth, then of course these should rise as well. How much they rise depends on the level of efficiency the company expects to achieve over time. Most publicly traded corporations will boast projected sales growth while purporting to trim operating expenses. In some instances, this might happen, but it is far from the norm.

Step Six.   Taxes should not be overlooked in the forecasting process. Clearly, they form a large part of any company's budget and should be treated accordingly. The estimated percentage that will be paid in taxes should be multiplied by pretax income. This amount is subtracted from pretax income to arrive at net income.

Step Seven.   With a complete income statement, you can begin to construct a cash flow statement. Normally, detailed cash flow projections would have to be crafted in tandem with balance sheet projections, which can be time-intensive, not to mention highly speculative. Specifically, estimating changes in accounts receivable, accounts payable, inventory, etc., can be painstakingly tedious. For this reason, many analysts prefer to look at simplified variations on cash flows such as EBITDA. By forecasting EBITDA, they are simply working from the income statement and, for the most part, producing numbers closer to cash. In some cases they subtract any extraordinary items such as capital expenditures, but in the end it begs the question, "Who really cares? These are all guesses anyway."

Summary. At this point, you can build out the cash flow and balance sheet changes. Usually, such models are dynamic and built into spreadsheets so that certain accounts will adjust automatically to reflect changes in other accounts.

To review, some of the items to build into your projections include the following:

- Accumulated depreciation
- Bad debt provisions
- Capital expenditures
- Changes in debt
- Depreciation rates
- Dividends
- Fixed-asset values
- General overhead
- Intangible assets
- Interest rates
- Inventory
- Material costs
- Research and development
- Sales volumes
- Selling and distribution costs
- Selling prices
- Share issues
- Tax rates

You can always come up with more, but these form a good starting point. Enjoy!

CHAPTER 6

Financial Analysis

In my early days of finance, I was given the opportunity to invest in one of two businesses. The first business was selling a branded product for which the demand was very high. The second was selling a product that the business both produced and sold to the consumer. The product, however, lacked brand appeal, something that inevitably leads to slower sales growth. While failing to do any further analysis, I chose to invest in the first company. I soon realized this was a big mistake, as the business eventually failed while the second went on to achieve remarkable success. But I learned a valuable lesson from this, something that Wall Street has been teaching for years and has stuck with me ever since. Basically, the numbers are good, but the analysis is better. Just because the sales numbers and profit numbers are strong does not mean that the company is. Or in this case, a business that posts meager results may in fact reveal untold future potential after some further analysis. A few of the following measures of financial analysis could have saved me from making a poor investment:

1. Profit margins
2. Sales growth projections
3. Return on equity
4. Inventory turnover

In fact, had I done this, I would have uncovered information that showed that the company I chose to invest in had:

1. Lower profit margins due to the high cost of acquiring the product
2. Slower sales growth due to increased competition in a crowded space
3. Lower return on equity due to multiple investors
4. Lower inventory turnover because management had overzealously ordered too much product to meet aggressive sales forecasts

To this day, I regret not investing in the second company, which performed exceptionally well. In fact, the founder earned the distinction of being called the Lemonade King in our neighborhood, while the company I invested in petered away like most of the other Kool-Aid stands on the block.

In this chapter, we will discuss the following:

- Financial statement analysis
- Trend analysis
- Ratio analysis
- EVA (economic value added)

Financial Statement Analysis

At this point, we transition to financial statement analysis. We have already taken a close look at the balance sheet, the income statement, and the cash flow statement. We saw that the balance sheet is essentially the doctor's report, because it tells us whether or not the company is in good financial health. We took a look at the income statement, which serves as the report card by helping to gauge the company's performance. Then, we took a look at the cash flow statement, which helps determine how much cash the company is generating. It serves as the checkbook for the company. Examining these statements is useful for making comparisons with prior years and, more importantly, with other companies. For that reason, there is an entire school of finance based on financial statement analysis. Wall Street research analysts, investment bankers, commercial bankers, financial managers, and traders commonly use this type of analysis. Nowadays, financial analysis has particular relevance as corporate managers are rewarded based on their ability to meet certain benchmarks. For example, a CEO's compensation will have some component dependent upon certain levels of quantifiable achievement that might include return on equity or profit margins. Furthermore, financial statement analysis can be useful in drawing performance comparisons between individual divisions of a company or between companies in an entire industry. Next, we will take a look at these techniques to understand what they are used for and who uses them.

Trend Analysis

One of the primary methods used to assess a company's performance is known as *trend analysis*. This takes on many different forms. The two most common methods are detailed here.

Year-to-Year Change Analysis

The most common way to assess a company's performance from one year to the next is called *year-to-year change analysis*. For example, look at a company's sales growth. If the company over time has grown its sales approximately 10% per year, that 10%

can be compared with the industry average. If the industry average reveals a trend whereby sales throughout the industry have grown at 20%, the conclusion can be drawn that the company has underperformed the industry. If, on the other hand, the industry trend is sales growth of 5%, the company seems to be doing reasonably well by outperforming the industry average. Year-to-year change analysis allows for the examination of virtually any item on the financial statements to determine a company's growth. From there, comparisons can be made with other items on the company's financials or with other companies in the industry.

Index-Number Trend-Series Analysis

Another method used to measure trends is called *index-number trend-series analysis*. This method is used for longer-term trend comparisons. It involves choosing a base year for all financial statement items and expressing each item, such as sales, as 100%. Every year after the base year, the sales number is adjusted above or below the base number to reflect the change. This process is helpful in assessing how these items have changed over an extended period of time.

	2000	2001	2003	2004	2005
Sales	100	150	175	200	250
Index-number trend	100%	150%	175%	200%	250%

Ratio Analysis

The most common method of analyzing companies is called *ratio analysis*. If you watch any of the stock investment shows, read Wall Street equity research reports, or work with bankers and accountants, you have probably encountered some type of ratio analysis. These ratios are helpful in determining the relative strength, performance, and value of a company. In fact, there are several different categories of ratios, each pertaining to a specific set of users. For example, operations managers will focus on performance activity. Short-term bank and trade creditors will focus on the immediate liquidity of the firm. Longer-term creditors, such as bondholders, will be interested in the long-term solvency of the firm. Managers will examine the profitability of the firm, whereas investors will monitor returns. Finally, market traders and equity analysts will be most interested in overall market performance. So for each group of financial professionals, there tends to be a corresponding set of ratios.

It is important to understand that ratio analysis helps provide an overall profile of a firm, its economic characteristics, and its competitive strategies. A primary advantage of ratio analysis is that it allows comparison among firms of different sizes. However, the construction of such ratios invariably involves a process of standardization; and in any such process, specific differences between the companies pertaining to capital structures, extraordinary items, and accounting methods tend to be ignored. For example, two very similar companies might use entirely different methods of calculating depreciation. If one uses a decelerated schedule and the other an accelerated one, the financial statements will reflect this; and more specifically, so will several profitability and asset-based ratios. The ratios themselves will not disclose this difference in accounting treatment, though the comparative analysis will certainly be affected.

So what can be done? It is unwise to completely disavow one of the fundamental tools of financial analysis (as tempting as that might seem). Rather, it is important to understand that one should not rely exclusively on ratio analysis to make a definitive conclusion about a company. Ratio analysis should be used as one part of the entire analysis process.

There are six broad categories of ratio analysis. Below is a brief description of each, along with the group that tends to use it:

1. *Activity analysis.* The first category is called *activity analysis*, which enables the evaluation of revenues and output generated by the firm's assets. Activity analysis is useful for operations managers as well as management consultants. In fact, a number of large consulting firms have built their practice around this type of ratio analysis.
2. *Liquidity analysis.* This measures the adequacy of the firm's cash resources and its ability to meet near-term cash obligations. Liquidity analysis is particularly useful for commercial bankers and, to a lesser degree, investment bankers, because it enables the lenders or the issuers to understand whether the firm has sufficient cash resources to meet the obligations of a particular offering.
3. *Long-term debt and solvency analysis.* This examines the company's capital structure, its mix of financing sources, and, more importantly, the ability of the firm to satisfy its longer-term debt and investment obligations. Investment bankers and fund managers often use this analysis.
4. *Profitability analysis.* This measures the income of the company relative to its revenues and invested capital. Profitability analysis is particularly useful for investment analysts, private equity investors, and, of course, the company managers themselves.
5. *Return analysis.* This examines the returns on assets, total capital, and equity in an effort to measure investment performance. Investors of any type use return analysis.

6. *Market analysis*. Finally, market analysis measures value, income, and dividends relative to one another. This is useful for investors and market traders.

Now let's examine each category in greater depth.

Activity Analysis

Activity analysis describes the relationship between a firm's level of operations and the assets needed to sustain these operating activities. It is helpful in assessing the overall efficiency of the business.

Inventory turnover days.   Inventory turnover days are a very common measure of a company's efficiency. This shows how frequently the company is converting its inventory to sale. This is important because inventory, to put it mildly, is costly for a number of reasons. On the one hand, there is a cost of storage. If the company produces or purchases inventory, it must store it. Whether the company owns its property or leases it, there will still be a cost associated with storage. The longer it takes to sell the inventory, the longer the company must store it and the more costly it becomes. At the same time, there are risks associated with inventory. Every time a piece of inventory is produced but not sold, the company faces the risk that eventually that inventory becomes obsolete. So the longer the inventory is held, the more likely it will end up liquidated at a discount or not sold at all. Also, the cost of financing inventory can create concerns for a company. The longer the inventory is held, the more the company assumes in financing costs. So there are numerous reasons why inventory is costly, and because of this, company managers will look at inventory turnover days.

$$\text{Inventory turnover days} = 365/(\text{cost of goods sold}/ \\ \text{average inventory})$$

As the formula above shows, inventory turnover days are calculated by taking 365 days in the year and dividing that number
by the ratio of cost of goods sold to average inventory. Suppose
a company has a cost of goods sold of $1 million and average
inventory of $100,000. We take the $1 million and divide it by
$100,000, which gives an inventory turnover of 10 times. In
other words, inventory turns over (sells) 10 times per year. Then
we divide that turnover of 10 into 365 days in the year to calculate inventory turnover days of 36.5. Based on this, we can con-
clude that every 36 to 37 days, inventory converts to sale. Is this
a good number? That depends. To decide, we measure this
against some industry average. If the industry average is 72 days,
36.5 days is a very good number, because competitors are taking
roughly double the amount of days to convert their inventory to
sale. If the industry average is 18, then 36.5 is not so strong.
Here competitors are converting their inventory in half the
amount of time.

Inventory turnover days are a useful measure because, as we
just saw, inventory is costly. The sooner inventory turns, the
better. In fact, inventory turnover becomes increasingly important in certain industries. One company in particular—see if
you guess which one—serves as a shining example of how far
inventory turnover can propel a business. This company maintained a relatively level stock price during the early part of the
new millennium while its competitors were observing precipi-
tous drops in share prices. Wall Street was quick to recognize
that this company's low inventory turnover days number was
freeing up cash and lowering the risk of excess inventory, both
serious concerns in an industry marked by new product innovations and liquidity problems. Give up? Dell Computer has a
world-class system of supply chain management that creates
numerous advantages in the process of inventory management.
By building computers to order, Dell maintains lower inventory

for a shorter period of time than most of its competitors. This lowers financing costs, storage costs, and obsolescence risk, all of which has helped Dell build billions of dollars in shareholder wealth.

Accounts receivable turnover days.   Like inventory, accounts receivable pose some concerns. Namely, the longer they remain outstanding, the more costly they become. The longer a company holds on to its receivables, the less likely it is to collect them. Furthermore, if there are receivables outstanding, the company is losing interest on those payments. To measure average collection rate, use accounts receivable turnover days.

$$\text{Accounts receivable turnover days} = 365/(\text{credit sales/average accounts receivable})$$

With accounts receivable turnover days, we take 365 days in a year and divide that number by the ratio of credit sales to average receivables. If the company has $1 million in credit sales and $100,000 in average receivables, the accounts receivable turnover days are 36.5—every 36 to 37 days, receivables convert to payment. Is this a good number? Again, it must be compared with the industry average. Now, this becomes an important measure in service industries because they are typically characterized by installment billing. Often, a service is performed with the expectation that payment will be received at some point in the future. Attorneys, accountants, physicians, and consultants spend a fair amount of time focused on collecting these payments. In corporate America, financial managers spend their time computing their accounts receivable turnover days.

Accounts payable turnover days.   The flip side of accounts receivable turnover days is accounts payable turnover days. This shows on average how long it takes the company to pay off its outstanding payables.

Accounts payable turnover days = 365/(purchases/average accounts payable)

To calculate this, take 365 days in the year and divide it by the ratio of purchases to average accounts payable. Purchases are defined as the cost of goods sold plus changes in inventory. So if the company has $1 million in purchases and $100,000 in average accounts payable, its accounts payable turnover days equals 36.5. Again, is this a good number? You know the answer. The idea here is to obtain as large a number as possible, because the longer the company has to turn over its payables, the better off it is—the longer it keeps that cash on hand. Of course, a lot of things can be done with that cash. The company can reinvest it or deploy it in some manner to create added benefit for the company. In theory, then, the longer it can hold on to the cash, the better off it is. However, the company does have to be careful not to overdo it. Too much of a good thing can cause problems. If analysts sense that this number is excessive, they may assume the company is facing liquidity problems.

Cash conversion cycle.   There is a formula that combines the different turnover numbers called the *cash conversion cycle* (CCC):

$$CCC = A/R \text{ days} + \text{inventory days} - A/P \text{ days}$$

As you can see, it is calculated by taking accounts receivable (A/R) days, plus inventory days, less accounts payable (A/P) days, and serves as a good measure of a company's immediate liquidity.

Averages.   The term *average* is prevalent throughout much of ratio analysis: *average inventory*, *average receivables*, and *average payables* are some of the more common ones. Each represents a balance sheet item, which, if you recall, reflects a snapshot at one particular point in time. For example, inventory would reflect the inventory at the end of the last reporting cycle. That may not accurately reflect what occurred during the reporting cycle, and therefore an average inventory number is needed. More often than not, that average number is calculated by taking the inventory number from the end of the most recent year plus the inventory number from the prior year and dividing the sum by 2. It is not perfect, but it works. A similar method of averaging can be used for any of the other balance sheet items when needed.

Liquidity Analysis

Liquidity analysis shows whether a company has sufficient liquid resources to cover its near-term obligations. This is something of particular interest to most commercial banks that often base their determination of a company's creditworthiness on these ratios.

Current ratio.   The first and most common measure of a company's liquidity is the current ratio.

Current ratio = current assets/current liabilities

The current ratio is calculated by dividing current assets by current liabilities. You might recall that current assets—which include cash, marketable securities, accounts receivable, and inventory—are those that can be converted to cash within a year and current liabilities are those that come due within a year. With the current ratio, the hope is that current assets will exceed current liabilities, resulting in a ratio greater than 1. This proves that the company has sufficient liquidity to cover its near-term obligations, which is a good position to be in. If current assets fall below current liabilities, the company would have a current ratio less than 1—and more importantly, a big problem on its hands. In other words, it does not have sufficient resources to cover its near-term obligations. In this case, the company could either sell off fixed assets or issue long-term debt. Either strategy would improve the current ratio. However, issuing more short-term debt would leave the company in a similarly weak position. While it would generate cash, it would commensurately boost current liabilities.

Quick ratio.   A variation on the current ratio is the quick ratio.

Quick ratio = (cash + marketable securities
                + accounts receivable)/current liabilities

The quick ratio adds cash, marketable securities, and accounts receivable and then divides the sum by current liabilities. The primary difference between the quick ratio and the current ratio is the exclusion of inventory in the quick ratio. For reasons discussed earlier, inventory is often seen as not truly liquid. It is difficult to sell and can eventually become obsolete. For that reason, many analysts believe the quick ratio is a better measure of a firm's immediate liquidity, because it uses a purer form of liquid assets.

Cash ratio.   The cash ratio adds cash to marketable securities and divides the sum by current liabilities.

Cash ratio = (cash + marketable securities)/current liabilities

With the cash ratio, both inventory and accounts receivable are excluded, because the view is that both are inherently problematic due to the difficulty in converting them to cash.

Long-Term Debt and Solvency Analysis

Long-term debt and solvency analysis is useful in determining if a company is optimally capitalized.

Debt-to-capital ratio.   The first and most common of these is what is called the *debt–to–total capital ratio* (*debt-to-cap ratio* in banker-speak). Investment bankers commonly use this to measure relative levels of debt. It is calculated by taking total debt (current debt plus long-term debt) and dividing it by the sum of total debt and total equity:

Debt-to-capital ratio = total debt/(total debt + total equity)

In other words, the debt-to-capital ratio measures debt outstanding relative to the company's entire capital structure. For example, a company's 50% debt-to-capital ratio could then be compared with an industry average. If the industry average is 20%, this company is clearly overleveraged. This proves useful in financing decisions, such as deciding on the appropriate mix of debt and equity financing. Investment bankers love the debt-to-capital ratio because they can tell their client either, "You're overleveraged; we should issue some equity to pay down that debt," or, "You're underleveraged; we should issue more debt." Either option results in hefty underwriting fees!

Debt-to-equity ratio.   The debt-to-equity ratio is a simple variation on the debt-to-capital ratio. Here, take total debt and divide it by total equity:

Debt to equity = total debt/total equity

Times interest earned ratio.   Finally, analysts use the times interest earned ratio, or what is commonly referred to as the *interest coverage ratio*. This is a popular measure not just in corporate finance, but in personal finance as well. If you have ever sought a loan of any type (e.g., home equity loan, school loan, auto loan), someone at some commercial bank took a look at your times interest earned ratio. The person who did this wanted to gauge your capacity to cover your interest expense. This was done by taking your earnings before interest and taxes and dividing it by your interest expense:

$$\text{Times interest earned} = \text{EBIT/interest}$$

The interest coverage ratio helps determine if a company has sufficient EBIT to cover the necessary interest payments on debt outstanding.

Profitability Analysis

Profitability analysis is an effective way of measuring the various levels of profits relative to sales. You might recall from Chapter 3, the chapter on the income statement, that companies exhibit different levels of profitability. Starting at the very top of the income statement, gross profit, EBIT, EBITDA, EBT, and net income are revealed. These levels of profitability are effective in measuring profitability among companies with varying operating and capital structures. This principle is observed in profitability ratios as well.

Gross margin.   Gross margin is the greatest ratio ever. It is hard to manipulate and offers an exceptional measure of a company's profitability at the highest level. It is calculated by taking gross profit and dividing it by sales:

$$\text{Gross margin} = \text{gross profit/sales}$$

Corporate managers are concerned with gross margin because the number is a measure of a company's distribution efficiency. Specifically, a company with higher gross margins derives more from a sale than one with lower margins even though their profits might be comparable. Investors prefer a company with a higher gross margin because this indicates stronger efficiency.

The best illustration of the importance of gross margins can be observed in the supermarket industry, which is generally characterized by low gross margins. In this industry, cost of goods sold tends to be very high relative to sales. An apple might cost the supermarket $0.32, while the supermarket might sell it for $0.35. Supermarkets, for that reason, are driven by volume. Additionally, a number of trends have emerged over the last decade to improve gross margins:

1. As supermarket chains consolidate, they are able to increase their buying power and, in turn, achieve better pricing from wholesalers. Additionally, by eliminating competition, prices may increase, further improving gross margins.
2. By diversifying into new products and services such as organic produce and banking services, supermarkets are able to capitalize on higher-margin offerings.

Additionally, consolidation among supermarket chains can lead to operating expense savings by eliminating overlapping functions. This will in turn boost other margins.

Operating margins.   The software industry is typically characterized by very high gross margins. Software traditionally exhibits these high gross margins because its cost of goods sold tends to be very low. The cost of goods sold for software is really the cost of disseminating it, either on disc or through Web-based applications. That tends to be a very small percentage of overall sales. In software, however, there are much higher operating expenses, which usually involve a significant amount of research and development. These expenses are distributed incrementally, or amortized, over some period of time. Research and development tends to be a large part of a software company's expense structure, so the company's operating margin is much lower. Operating margin pertains to operating income divided by sales:

$$\text{Operating margin} = \text{operating income/sales}$$

Profit margin. Finally, the most common measure of profitability is the profit margin, net income divided by sales:

$$\text{Profit margin} = \text{net income/sales}$$

Return Analysis

Return analysis is frequently referred to as *return on investment* (ROI), a very common term used by investment managers. "What is the ROI on this investment?" is a question often heard within the walls of venture capital firms. ROI can be calculated a number of different ways.

Return on assets. Return on assets is calculated by taking net income and dividing it by total assets:

$$\text{Return on assets} = \text{net income/total assets}$$

Return on total capital. Another way to calculate return on investment is by calculating return on total capital. Here, net income is divided by the sum of total debt plus total equity:

$$\text{Return on total capital} = \text{net income/(total debt} + \text{total equity)}$$

Return on equity. Finally, ROI can be calculated as return on equity. This is done by taking net income and dividing it by total equity (shareholders' equity):

$$\text{Return on equity} = \text{net income/total equity}$$

Market Analysis

Lastly, there is a category known as *market analysis*. If you have ever seen an investment show or if you follow the market, you will probably be familiar with one or more of the terms described below. They are useful for gauging stock price performance, dividend payout, and valuation. These ratios are used commonly by Wall Street traders as well as mom-and-pop investors. This information used to be part of an esoteric language spoken by the so-called industry analysts and experts. Nowadays, though, with the advent of the Internet, this information is much more readily available.

Price-to-earnings ratio.   The first of the market ratios is the price-to-earnings ratio, or the P/E ratio. The P/E ratio is useful because it enables the analyst to gauge the relative value of a company. It is measured by dividing the company's stock price by its earnings per share:

Price-to-earnings ratio = stock price/earnings per share

The share price of a company's stock reflects the company's ability to generate profits. The P/E ratio reveals the price that an investor must pay to capture a dollar of earnings. A company's P/E ratio is measured relative to an industry average or peer group. If the P/E ratio of a company exceeds the P/E ratio of the industry, it is usually determined that the company is overvalued. If the P/E ratio of the company is less than the industry average, it is observed that the company might be undervalued. And if the P/E ratio of the company is equal to the industry average, the company is probably fairly valued.

As mentioned earlier, ratios should seldom form the sole evaluation criterion. Rather, they should be used in conjunction with much more detailed analysis. They're merely a starting point.

However, in many, many instances the P/E ratio is useful for valuation purposes.

There are instances when the P/E has fallen below the market average for good reason and the company is not considered undervalued. For example, a company that is awaiting the ruling in a lawsuit that could be potentially unfavorable would probably exhibit a lower P/E ratio than the market average.

Suppose a company has a market price per share of $20. If this company has earnings per share of $2, its price-to-earnings ratio is 10. If the industry average is 15, then the company is probably undervalued. Again there could be reasons for this, but at first glance, it appears that the company is undervalued. Now if the industry average is 7, the company might be seen as overvalued.

Earnings yield.   Earnings yield takes earnings per share and divides it by the market price per share. It's the inverse of the P/E ratio or, in other words, the earnings you buy with a dollars' worth of stock.

Earnings yield = earnings per share/market price per share

So if the company has earnings per share of $2 and a market price per share of $20, its earnings yield is 10%.

Dividend yield.   Dividend yield takes dividends per share and divides them by market price per share. This helps assess how much the company is paying in dividends relative to its market price per share, or what percentage of the market price is that dividend. Also, that can be compared with an industry average to see if the company is paying more or less than the industry average.

Dividend yield = dividends per share/market price per share

If the company pays out $1 in dividends with a market price per share of $20, the dividend yield is 5%. If the industry average is 10%, the company is paying less than the industry. Is that a good yield? Since dividends tend to be one of the more controversial topics in finance, this is difficult to determine. There are those who believe that dividends should be paid out regularly and those who believe that they tend to compromise company growth. When a dividend is paid out, it represents the loss of funds that could have been used to grow the company through research, development, new product launches, and acquisitions. Certain companies consistently pay out very strong dividends and are praised for that, while other companies pay out little or no dividends and have performed reasonably well using this model.

Dividend payout ratio.   The dividend payout ratio takes dividends per share and divides them by earnings per share:

$$\text{Dividend payout ratio} = \text{dividends per share}/\text{earnings per share}$$

So if a company pays out $1 in dividends and has $2 in earnings, its dividend payout ratio is 50%. Again, whether this is a good or a bad number depends on industry averages. If the company pays out a dividend of $1 per share and has earnings per share of $2, its dividend payout ratio is 50%. The remaining $1 is then transferred back to the balance sheet in the form of retained earnings.

Price-to-book ratio.   Finally, the price-to-book ratio takes market price per share and divides it by book price per share:

$$\text{Price-to-book ratio} = \text{market price per share}/\text{book price per share}$$

Market price per share is the price observed in the open market. For a publicly traded company, this is the stock price. The book price per share is the price or the value observed on the balance sheet, listed as owners' equity, and is not usually considered a good indicator of company value. Market value is based on the demand for the company or its shares, and it is commonly accepted as a starting point in the sale process. Rarely are these two numbers the same. Usually market price will exceed book price, though there are instances when these two numbers converge, which is often seen as a buying opportunity. In fact, many private equity investors will look for these rare instances because they seek to acquire companies for very little, restructure them, and resell them at a higher value. Through these acquisitions and restructurings, significant value is unlocked, creating a strong return on investment and, in turn, a higher price-to-book ratio.

EVA

Economic value added, or EVA, is a relatively recent performance measure developed to help companies calculate their true economic profit. One of the major advantages of EVA is that it can be used to measure performance on a divisional level, unlike other methods of analysis and valuation. EVA essentially does this by taking net operating profits after taxes less a charge for the opportunity cost of invested capital. In other words, it measures a company's performance after deducting its cost of capital from its tax-adjusted operating profit. Some uses for EVA include:

- Strategic goal setting
- Bonus determination
- Capital budgeting
- Valuation
- Equity analysis

The derivation of the formula for EVA is as follows:

Net sales − operating expenses = operating profit

Operating profit − taxes = net operating profit after taxes

Net operating profit after taxes − capital charges
(capital × cost of capital) = EVA

Or simply put:

EVA = net operating profit after taxes
− (capital × cost of capital)

EVA seeks to measure profitability after a company accounts for its cost of invested capital. This capital charge is what really drives the EVA analysis. Although the company is seemingly profitable, it must exceed the cost of capital to truly benefit the shareholders. Suppose you manage a large, multidivisional, multinational corporation. EVA provides a useful and user-friendly performance measure. You can measure EVA based on operating divisions or even on a regional basis. It is a simple standard that most shareholders can understand, and aside from the cost of capital, it is rarely subject to manipulation. Although EVA is gaining ground in application, it still has a ways to go before becoming universally accepted.

PART II

FINANCE

CHAPTER 7

Cost of Capital

At this point, you have made it reasonably far into this book and are feeling pretty good about yourself. That's all fine and dandy, but no good book on financial concepts would be complete without a section that causes you to rethink your intellect—and more importantly, your value as a contributing member of society. For that reason, I give you cost of capital.

Almost everyone has a friend who only dates people who are volatile and high risk. When things are good, they're really good. And when things are bad, they're really bad. The relationship is a veritable roller coaster with constant highs and lows. And, of course, almost everyone has a friend who only dates people who are stable, secure, and low risk. Monotony and routine supersede excitement and thrills. For the former, payoffs can be huge or they can be disastrous. And for the latter, payoffs are usually adequate. In the world of finance, we use the term *cost of capital* to measure payoffs and risk.

You will hear the term *cost of capital* quite a bit in financial circles, and yet it is rarely explained. So what is the cost of capital? That depends on the context. For example, a simple definition pertains to the rate required or charged for the use of funds. If you go to the bank and take out a loan, your cost of that loan is what you pay in interest. So interest rates are a good example of a cost of capital. Now you can look at a related concept, the opportunity cost of capital, which is the rate of return offered by equivalent investment alternatives in the capital market—essentially the cost of capital based on the opportunity that's forgone. The opportunity cost of capital is also referred to as the *discount rate* or the *hurdle rate*.

Consider the following:

- You invest $100,000 today into Project A.
- Project B, an ongoing project, is equally as risky as Project A.
- Project B's expected rate of return one year from today is 20%.
- If you invested $90,000 in Project B today, based on historical performance, you would expect to have $108,000 one year from now (you earned 20% on that $90,000 investment).
- What is the opportunity cost of capital if you invested in Project A?

Your opportunity cost of capital would be 20%, which is the expected return from the investment opportunity forgone from Project B. Therefore the expected payoff from Project A would be $100,000 times 120%, giving you a total of $120,000 (by applying that 20% opportunity cost of capital to Project A).

In practice, investors do not normally know what the exact return on a project is, but they will use a benchmark on an equally risky investment to help calculate another project's expected return. The cost of capital measures the amount charged for the use of funds, and it is usually expressed in annual percentage terms. The opportunity cost of capital measures the opportunity forgone by investing in a project of similar risk.

The question now arises: how do you decide upon that appropriate opportunity cost of capital? Opportunity cost of capital depends on the risk involved in the project. In fact, investors will typically expect a higher rate of return if they deem a project to be riskier than any other opportunity in the market. The simple reason for this is that they want to be compensated for the higher risk involved. This has been observed throughout history. In the 1980s, corporations issued high-yield "junk" bonds to fund risky projects. By assuming an excessively high level of risk, the bondholders were paid a commensurately high rate of interest because they were to be compensated accordingly for the extra risk. Namely, they were compensated for the possibility that the project might not come to fruition, or might dissolve altogether, in which case they would lose their entire investment.

Before we take a look at calculating the cost of capital, ponder a final question: why the heck do we even care about the cost of capital? Cost of capital is useful in the world of finance for two primary reasons:

1. It serves as an effective performance benchmark.
2. It enables the calculation of present values of future payments—something extremely useful in valuation analysis.

As a performance benchmark, cost of capital is useful in determining how much a company must earn on its assets to meet the expectations of investors and creditors. For example, if a company's cost of capital is 18%, then any return above 18% will serve to enhance the company's perception and, hopefully, value. In other words, a company that returns in excess of its cost of capital should see an increase in stock price. Logically, this makes sense, because any excess over what was expected should serve to attract new investors. The price should continue to rise until it reflects the company's cost of capital, which in this case is 18%. Conversely, a company that underperforms its cost of capital should in turn see a share price adjustment downward to reflect this.

As a valuation variable, cost of capital will affect the overall value of a company when based on future returns (i.e., cash flows, EBITDA, etc.). This will be covered in much more detail in Chapter 8 on valuation, where the cost of capital will be related to what is commonly termed the *discount rate*. In this chapter, we will discuss the following:

- Cost of equity
- Weighted-average cost of capital

Cost of Equity

The cost of equity is essentially the return expected by the shareholders of the company. Unlike debt, where the debt holders are promised a certain rate, equity offers no clearly defined return. As such, there are several ways to calculate this. The two methods examined here are among those more commonly used by Wall Street analysts and bankers. The first is called the *dividend growth model*, and the second is called the *capital asset pricing model*, or what is commonly referred to as the *CAPM*.

Dividend Growth Model

The dividend growth model is considered the easiest way to estimate the cost of equity capital. It is predicated on the notion that the firm's dividend will grow at a constant rate. The dividend growth model is written as follows:

$$r_E = (D_1/P_0) + g$$

where

r_E = return on equity (cost of equity)

$D_1 = D_0 \times (1 + g)$

D_0 = most recent dividend payment

P_0 = current stock price

g = estimated dividend growth (use historical rates or analysts forecasts)

As you can see, in this model, the return on equity (r_E), or the cost of equity, is equal to the dividend after the first period (D_1) divided by the current stock price (P_0), which is then added to the growth rate (g).

To better understand the model, we must review the components in more detail. The first component, the dividend after the first period, is calculated by taking the last or most recent dividend payment (D_0) and multiplying it by 1 plus the growth rate. The stock price is the current market price per share, and the growth rate is the estimated dividend growth.

There are a couple of ways to estimate dividend growth. One method is to simply look at historical rates and take an average of the last several years. Another method involves analysts' forecasts for the company, or might even involve that of the entire industry.

To better understand this, look at the sample problem below:

A utility company paid a dividend of $2 per share last year, which is expected to grow at 6% per year indefinitely. If the company has a current share price of $60, what would its return on equity be, based on the dividend growth model?

Apply the dividend growth formula to the sample problem here. This company paid a dividend of $2 per share last year, and the company is expected to grow the dividend at a rate of 6%

per year for the foreseeable future. With the shares of the company at $60, calculate its return on equity or cost of equity based on the dividend growth model.

To begin, calculate D_1 by taking the most recent dividend payment, $D_0 = \$2$, and increasing it by the growth rate of 6%, which equals $2.12 ($2 × 1.06 = $2.12). Then, take that $2.12 and divide it by the company's share price of $60 to get 3.5%. Next, add that to the growth rate of 6% to arrive at 9.5%. Thus, as determined by a the dividend growth model, the cost of equity is 9.5%. The advantage of this model is primarily its simplicity. However, a number of problems arise from this approach. For one, it is only applicable to companies that pay dividends. Furthermore, these dividends must grow at a constant rate, and the result is highly sensitive to this growth rate. Finally, risk, which is a key measure of return on equity, is not explicitly considered. So to account for these shortcomings, an alternative method— the capital asset pricing model—is often used to calculate the cost of equity.

Capital Asset Pricing Model

The capital asset pricing model, or the CAPM, is useful in measuring the cost of equity because it measures risk explicitly. It is also applicable to companies that may not have steady dividend growth. In its simplest form, the CAPM states that the expected return on a stock is the sum of the rate of return on a risk-free security and some expected risk premium rate. This is usually measured in correlation to the market risk premium.

It is important to understand that the CAPM is defined in terms of expectations, and as such, investors are compensated in the expected sense. Actual returns will typically deviate from these expectations, but they form a useful estimation. The CAPM prices securities relative to their market risk premium, meaning that market risk is a key input in this process. The expected risk premium on a security is proportional to the risk premium expected on the overall market.

At this point, you should be entirely confused. The CAPM is fairly difficult to grasp initially, but with some work, it should become manageable soon. Here is the formula for the CAPM:

$$r_E = r_f + \beta(r_m - r_f)$$

The expected rate of return, or the return on equity (r_E), is equal to the risk-free rate (r_f) plus beta (β) multiplied by the return on the market (r_m) less the risk-free rate. Or perhaps it is better explained as the sum of the risk-free rate plus some risk premium associated with that particular security. The individual components are discussed below.

Risk-free rate. How is a risk-free security defined? A risk-free security is a security whose rate of return is guaranteed. Specifically, there is no risk of default on these payments because the payments have no associated risks aside from inflation. Typical risk-free securities are government securities, such as Treasury bills, Treasury notes, and Treasury bonds. Usually, Treasury bills are considered the safest because they have very little to no interest rate fluctuation risk, unlike their T-note and T-bond counterparts. These securities are considered risk-free because the U.S. government has never defaulted on its debt . . . at least not yet. So a good risk-free rate would be the rate on Treasury bills.

Market rate. To better understand the market rate, it is necessary to understand the concept of a market portfolio. A market portfolio is designed to cover all the risky securities in the market or to be a representation of the risky securities in that market. This provides a clear benchmark for overall market performance. A typical market portfolio would be the S&P 500 Index. Although only 500 companies are included in this index out of several thousand publicly traded companies, these 500 account for a substantial portion of the value of all stocks traded. For that reason, the S&P 500 Index is often used to represent the market portfolio. So the market rate would be based on this.

Beta. Ah, beta. Many use it but few understand it, and that is quite alright. In fact, I have yet to meet an investment banker who can derive beta. Beta measures the correlation of the returns on individual stocks relative to the returns on the overall market. It is assumed that the beta of the overall market is 1. This is because the market is the portfolio of all stocks, and so the average stock should have a beta of 1. Stocks with betas greater than 1 would tend to amplify market movements. Stocks with betas between zero and 1 would tend to move in the same direction as the market, but not by as much. For example, assume that the market returns 10%. A stock whose beta is 1.5 would return 15%, because it would go up 1½ times as much as the market. Suppose this stock has a beta of 0.5. If the market goes up 10%, this stock would go up 5% because it would move by half as much as the market.

Beta is derived through some complex calculations. Statisticians and some portfolio managers will actually calculate beta by taking the covariance between the return on the stock and the overall market and dividing it by the variance on the overall market return:

$$\beta = \sigma_s \sigma_m / \sigma_m^2$$

where

$\sigma_s \sigma_m$ = covariance between the return on stock S and
the overall market return

σ_m^2 = variance of the market return

These are challenging concepts that you should not worry yourself over. In fact, beta can usually be found easily on virtually any financial Web site or in any number of publications. If you are interested in calculating beta, please take the quiz below to determine if you are qualified:

Have you ever been to a *Star Trek* convention?   Y   N
Are you fluent in Wookie or Ewok?   Y   N
Did your college alma mater name include "Tech"?   Y   N
Do you value your friends based on the number of computer languages in which they can program?   Y   N
Do you read comic books?   Y   N
Do you wear a pocket protector?   Y   N
Have you ever received a wedgie?   Y   N
Do you prefer calculus problems over crossword puzzles?   Y   N
Did you actually buy this book?   Y   N

If you answered yes to any of these, you are probably qualified to calculate beta. Take a moment to review your understanding of beta with a couple of questions below.

Q: If a company has a beta of 1.5, is it riskier or less risky than the market?

A: *Technically it would be riskier because it tends to amplify the overall market movements.*

Q: Suppose another company has a beta of 0.8. Is it riskier or less risky than the market?

A: *It would be slightly less risky.*

Finally, take a moment to set up the capital asset pricing model and calculate the expected rate of return on stock S (r_S), using the following information:

Risk-free rate of return (r_f) = 4%
β of stock S = 1.2
Rate of return on market (r_m) = 7%

Plug those numbers into the CAPM formula:

$$r_S = r_f + β(r_m - r_f)$$
$$r_S = 4\% + 1.2(7\% - 4\%)$$
$$r_S = 7.6\%$$

As you can see, to calculate the rate of return on stock S, take the risk-free rate of 4% and add it to the result of a beta of 1.2 multiplied by the difference between the return on the market of 7% and the risk-free rate of 4%. What you get is 7.6%, the return on equity for stock S.

In the example below, you can calculate the beta of stock X using the capital asset pricing model. Here, you might use the resulting beta as a proxy for that of a similar company. For this example, the risk-free rate of return is 5%, the return on the market is 13%, and the rate of return on stock X is 6.9%. For quick reference, set up the "givens" this way:

Risk-free rate of return (r_f) = 5%
Rate of return on market portfolio (r_m) = 13%
Rate of return on stock X (r_X) = 6.9%

Once again, plug the numbers into the CAPM formula:

$$r_X = r_f + β(r_m - r_f)$$
$$6.9\% = 5\% + β(13\% - 5\%)$$
$$β = 0.24$$

What you did here was to set the return on stock X, 6.9%, equal to the rest of the equation, which included the risk-free rate of 5% plus beta, which you were solving for, multiplied by the return on the market of 13% less the risk-free rate of 5%. If you work backward through that and solve for beta, you arrive at something that is roughly 0.24. So if the market goes up 10%, this particular stock's return would be about 2.4%. More importantly, this can be applied to a company that behaves in a similar manner.

At this point, it should be clear that risk is proportional to expected return on a security. The capital asset pricing model is predicated on this relationship between risk and the expected rate of return. The basic benchmark for the CAPM formula is the risk-free rate, which is usually tied to Treasury bills. Now, the CAPM assumes that if a company has debt in its capital structure, any risk associated with the security on that debt is already priced into its beta. So what does that translate to? It essentially means that we are making some loose assumptions here about debt, and therefore the CAPM is really only useful insofar as we are looking at equity. It more or less accounts for the risk associated with equity.

Weighted-Average Cost of Capital

To reach an assessment on what the overall cost of capital is for a firm, you must use what is called the *weighted-average cost of capital* (WACC). This is the most common method used to measure the overall cost of capital. The major advantage of the weighted-average cost of capital, or the WACC, is that it takes into account financing decisions—namely, the mix of debt and equity, and more specifically, their weighted averages. Furthermore, the WACC also takes into account the fact that interest payments are tax deductible, and therefore it is important to look at it on an after-tax basis.

How does this work? Suppose a company issues debt and pays a 10% coupon on that debt. If this company is in a 30% tax bracket, what would its after-tax cost of debt be? Given the fact that the interest payments are tax deductible, the after-tax cost of debt in this case would actually be 7%:

$$\text{After-tax cost of debt} = r(1 - T)$$

where

r = coupon rate
T = tax rate

The weighted-average cost of capital takes this into consideration, with tax affecting the debt interest. The weighted-average cost of capital looks like this:

$$r_{\text{WACC}} = (1 - T)r_D D/V + r_E E/V$$

where

T = tax rate
r_D = rate of return on debt (usually the yield and not the coupon rate)
D = total debt outstanding
V = total capital of the company $(D + E)$
r_E = rate of return on equity
E = market value of equity

As the equation above shows, the weighted-average cost of capital is equal to 1 minus the tax rate, multiplied by the rate of return on the debt multiplied by the ratio of the total debt outstanding to the total capital of the company. This is then added to the return on equity multiplied by the ratio of equity to the total capital of the company.

Capital structure here is denoted by V, and that represents debt outstanding plus the market value of equity. The return on equity can be calculated using what has already been covered, either the dividend discount model or the capital asset pricing model. Some analysts will use both and take an average; others, when possible, will simply use the capital asset pricing model because it tends to be a bit more detailed and is perceived as being more credible.

Generally speaking, the weighted-average cost of capital is the preferred method of all cost of capital measures. It takes into account the firm's overall capital structure as well as the tax benefits or the tax deductibility of interest.

In the next example you also solve for the weighted-average cost of capital. In this example, the return on debt of 9%, the tax rate of 35%, and the ratio of debt to overall capital structure of 30% are all given. Return on equity has already been calculated at 15% using the dividend growth model. Succinctly, written, we have:

$r_D = 9\%$
$T = 35\%$
$D/V = 30\%$
$r_E = 15\%$ (assume this was already calculated using the dividend growth model)

We are new ready to set up the formula for the weighted-average cost of capital and then substitute:

$$r_{WACC} = (1 - T)r_D(D/V) + r_E(E/V)$$
$$= (1 - 0.35)0.09(0.3) + 0.15(0.7)$$
$$= 0.1226, \text{ or } 12.26\%$$

(Note that $E/V = 1 - D/V$
$$= 1 - 0.3$$
$$= 0.7 \text{ (or } 70\%), \text{ because } V = D + E.)$$

So in solving this problem, first take 1 minus the tax rate of 35%, which is then multiplied by the weighted-average cost of capital return on debt of 9%, multiplied by the ratio of debt to the overall capital structure of the company of 30%. This is then added to the return on equity of 15%, which is multiplied by the ratio of equity to the overall capital structure of the company of 70%. This is an additional calculation that had to be made, because the value for E, the value of equity, was not given. The total value (V) of the company is composed of total debt (D) and total equity (E). So if 30% of the company is debt, the other 70% is presumed equity. After inserting all these variables, the end result is a weighted-average cost of capital of 12.26%.

As shown earlier, return on equity can be calculated either through the dividend growth model or through the capital asset pricing model. In this next example, calculate the weighted-average cost of capital using the following information: a return on debt of 8%, a tax rate of 35%, an equity to capital structure of 40%, a beta of 1.2, a risk-free rate of 6%, and a return on the market of 14%.

$r_D = 8\%$
$T = 35\%$
$E/V = 40\%$
$\beta = 1.2$
$r_f = 6\%$
$r_m = 14\%$

Given this information, it is clear that the capital asset pricing model needs to be employed to solve for the equity component. The first step is to use the capital asset pricing model to find the return on equity. Once you have the return on equity, you can plug that number into the weighted-average cost of capital model.

First, calculate r_E using the CAPM formula:

$$r_E = r_f + \beta \, (r_m - r_f)$$
$$= 0.06 + 1.2(0.14 - 0.06)$$
$$= 0.156, \text{ or } 15.6\%$$

You were given the risk-free rate of 6%, which you added to a beta of 1.2, which was multiplied by the difference between the return on the market and the risk-free rate, 14% less 6%. The end result is a return on equity of 15.6%.

Next, plug in r_E and calculate after-tax WACC:

$$r_{\text{WACC}} = (1 - T)r_D(D/V) + r_E(E/V)$$
$$= (1 - 0.35)0.08(0.6) + 0.156(0.4)$$
$$= 0.0936, \text{ or } 9.36\%$$

(Note that $D/V = 1 - E/V$
$$= 1 - 0.4$$
$$= 0.6 \text{ (or 60\%), because } V = D + E.)$$

The first thing done with the weighted-average cost of capital model was to take 1 minus the tax rate of 35%, multiplied by the return on debt of 8%, multiplied by the ratio of debt to the overall capital structure of 60%. Then, that was added to the return on equity derived above of 15.6%, multiplied by the ratio of equity to overall capital structure. In solving those numbers you come up with a weighted-average cost of capital of 9.36%, which is the discount rate or the number you use to discount future cash flows to find their present value. (We will see how discount rates are used in Chapter 8, "Valuation.")

Finally, here is another weighted-average cost of capital problem where the following information is given. This company has debt outstanding of $75 million. This company has return on debt of 9%. Its equity outstanding is 2 million shares at $42 per share. Calculate the return on equity given the following assumptions—assumptions that feed into the dividend growth model. The historic dividend is $5. The price per share is $37.14, and the growth rate is 4%. Last, but not least, the tax rate is 35%.

First, set up the assumptions so you can see them at a glance:

Debt outstanding = $75 million
$r_D = 9\%$
Equity outstanding = 2 million shares at $42 per share

r_E = use the dividend growth model assuming:

$$D_0 = \$5$$
$$P_0 = \$37.14$$
$$g = 4\%$$

Tax rate = 35%

In this example, first calculate the return on equity using the dividend growth model. After plugging these numbers into that equation, a return on equity of 18% is determined. Then plug that 18% into the weighted-average cost of capital. So take 1 minus the tax rate of 35%, multiply it by the return on debt of 9%, which is then multiplied by the ratio of debt to the overall capital structure of 47%. Now, this was solved by looking at the firm's capital structure. It has $75 million of debt and $84 million of equity, which is 2 million times $42 per share. So the debt component of that is 47%. We then add that to the return on equity that was derived, 18%, multiplied by the ratio of equity to the overall capital structure of 53%. Finally, multiply this by the return on equity of 18% and then solve the equation to come up with 12.29%, the weighted-average cost of capital. That is the discount rate that would be used to discount the future cash flows for this company.

$$r_E = \$5.2/\$37.14 + 0.04$$
$$= 0.14 + 0.04$$
$$= 0.18, \text{ or } 18\%$$

$$r_{WACC} = (1 - 0.35)(0.09)(0.47) + (0.18)(0.53)$$
$$= 0.12289, \text{ or } 12.29\%$$

In the next chapter, you will see just how important the cost of capital is when valuing companies.

CHAPTER 8

Valuation

One of my first lessons on Wall Street was that to get ahead, you had to be creative. What I noticed was that successful investment bankers had a real knack for making something out of nothing. For example, when numbers didn't look just right, a good banker could always tweak them a bit. No matter what a client desired—a higher selling price, a lower purchase price, stronger margins, lower capital costs, you name it—the banker could produce the numbers. A really good banker would earn the title of "numerical masseuse," and if you could send a masseuse to value a company, watch out!

The principles covered in this section apply not only to large corporate transactions, but to simple personal finance dealings as well. Such principles lead to methodologies for valuing companies and opportunities. There are numerous ways to value a company. Some include adjusted net assets, capitalization of earnings, dividend-paying capacity, excess earnings return on assets, and specific industry formulas. In fact, I could easily furnish you with a list of 40 or 50 such methods, and indeed, most have some relevance in certain situations. However, only a few have proved themselves to be credible, and those are the ones explained in this book.

Back in the mid-nineties, there was a strong movement to value Internet and software companies. The problem was that these companies were losing money and had very little prospect of ever making money. Nonetheless, many Wall Street analysts sought to formulate some method of valuation for them. Eventually, several clever equity analysts developed a hybrid form of ratio analysis by using price-to-sales ratios. The problem with these is that just because a company is generating sales does not necessarily mean that it is generating profits, and a company that does not generate profits will not be around very long. Hence, most of these methodologies have proved problematic, and as such, they are no longer around, much like the companies they were developed for!

Of the myriad ways to value a company, only a handful have withstood the test of time and proved credible across industries. In this chapter, we will discuss the following:

- Valuation basics
- Methods of valuation
- Net present value

Valuation Basics

You might recall the following facts from grade school:

- The island of Manhattan was purchased from the Manhattes Indians for $24 worth of trinkets in 1626.
- The Louisiana Territory was purchased from the French for $11 million in 1803.
- Alaska was purchased from the Russians for $7.2 million in 1867.

What do all these have in common? If you answered that each represents an effective use of economic imperialism as a means to emerge as a formidable competitor to the established European hegemony, well, you get an A in political science. Unfortunately, this is finance, and so you would fail. You should have said that each purchase was a good deal for the acquiring government. Or was it? This would all depend on what rate these amounts could have earned in competing investments. For example, $24 invested at a rate of 4% in 1626 would be worth about $70 million today. However, that same amount invested in 1626 at a rate of 8% would be worth over $100 trillion. The point of all this is that money spent yesterday has a different value today and will have a different value tomorrow. These values can change drastically, depending on the numbers used in calculating them. This is a fundamental principle in finance.

Time Value of Money

Before examining methods of valuation, it is essential to review a fundamental concept in finance known as the *time value of money*. The time value of money states that $1 received today has a different value from $1 received a year ago, or from $1 received a year from now. For example, a firm receives a $100 payment on January 1. It then deposits this payment into an interest-bearing account, one that pays 5%. On December 31 that account is now worth $105. It earned 5% interest, or $5.

Now, take that a step further. Suppose the firm was owed $100 on January 1 but was not paid until December 31. The value of that expected receipt is now less because of the forgone interest. In the course of that year, the expected receipt has diminished in value. How much less or what that new value is can be calculated using the present value formula.

Present Value

Present value is the concept that money spent tomorrow must be worth less today because of the time value of money. The present value amount is calculated with the formula:

$$PV = CF/(1 + r)^n$$

where

PV = present value
CF = cash flow for the period
r = discount rate
n = period

If you are like me and the majority of my students, this can be somewhat daunting at first glance. What this formula shows is the value of something paid tomorrow in today's values. As noted, CF stands for cash flow for the period, or the payment that is expected in the future. That payment is divided by $1 + r$ raised to the n power, with r standing for the discount rate and n representing the future period. When valuing cash flows received one year from now, $n = 1$. When valuing cash flows five years from now, $n = 5$. The discount rate in this context is based on the cost of capital, which was covered in the last chapter.

In the example from above, the firm is owed $100 on January 1 but is not paid until December 31. If the discount rate (r) is 5% and the period (n) is one year, calculate the present value of the $100:

$$PV = CF/(1 + r)^n$$
$$= \$100/(1 + 5\%)^1$$
$$= \$100/1.05$$
$$= \$95.24$$

So the present value of that $100 payment is only $95.24. If the firm had received $95.24 on January 1 and deposited it into an interest-bearing account, it would have $100 on December 31.

Methods of Valuation

If there is one thing that years of work in the field of valuation has taught me, it is that valuation is far more of an art than a science. In fact, I would go so far as to say that it is far more three-card monte than science. Don't get me wrong. I've spent the better part of my career working to effectively "value" projects; but at the same time, I'm the first to admit that there is only one true value of a company: what the buyer and seller agree on.

When you spot what appears to be framed smears of finger paint on your friend's wall and wonder, "Wow, I can't believe he spent $1 million on something a child could do," you might not be alone in your thinking. However, art collectors like your friend have created a market for such paintings, and more specifically, have set their value. Regardless of your opinion, the value of that work is $1 million because that is what the buyer and seller agreed on.

The world of finance takes this principle fairly seriously. However, oftentimes some dialogue needs to first be generated between prospective buyers and sellers. These methods of valuation enable this to occur. By creating detailed valuation models, the key factors that drove a company in the past, along with those that will continue to drive it in the future, can be examined. Both sides are able to form a better picture of the potential as well as the risks associated with this company. Through this process of dialogue, they will hopefully build some consensus. Then, with a little luck, they just might close a sale. This process can be engaged when buying companies outright, investing in them, restructuring them, etc. In fact, there are numerous uses for valuation. A few of the more common ones are listed here:

- Venture capital
- Initial public offerings

- Mergers and acquisitions
- Leveraged buyouts
- Estate and tax settlements
- Divorce settlements
- Capital raising
- Partnerships
- Restructurings
- Real estate
- Joint ventures
- Project finance

Now, even if you have no dealings in these types of transactions, and more specifically, no interest in them, it is important to at least have a basic understanding of the underlying principles and techniques of valuation. Why? Because so much of what we do and so much of what governs our personal lives is driven by these principles. The simple decision to lease or buy a car is driven by valuation. The decision to own or rent an apartment is driven by valuation. Changes in the stock market that might affect your job are a function of valuation. Get the picture? It is important that each one of us understand the basics of valuation because we can no longer rely on the experts on Wall Street, in corporate America, and at the big accounting firms. We have seen what can happen when we place absolute trust in them. In fact, it is easy to point fingers at these institutions for the financial catastrophes that have occurred throughout history. Ultimately, though, we all bear some responsibility because we were the ones who failed to educate ourselves. So now is our chance. We are ready to dive headfirst into the financial abyss (or pool, depending on our objectives) by working with these various methods of valuation.

Replacement Method

The replacement method of valuation tends to be the simplest to explain but the most time consuming to produce. It is based on a target company or asset that is valued by estimating the cost to create an exact duplicate. In other words, it seeks an answer to the question, "What would this cost to build from scratch?" To explore the answer, let's return to our favorite hardware store.

In the case of Cunningham Hardware, this method would measure all the costs involved in creating a duplicate store. These costs might include:

- Land
- Buildings
- Machinery
- Equipment
- Working capital

These costs are summed and then used as a proxy for fair value of the asset or business. Major drawbacks include difficulty in gathering complete information, and more importantly, difficulty valuing intangibles such as brand name, intellectual property, or perhaps customer loyalty.

In the case of Cunningham Hardware, suppose the following costs are needed to re-create a comparable store:

Land	$150,000
Building	$280,000
Computers and computer systems	$40,000
Inventory	$60,000
Hiring and training costs	$10,000
Legal costs	$5,000
Additional start-up costs	$8,000

Once these costs are totaled, a fair value of $553,000 is determined. Of course, this fails to consider the name that Cunningham has built, its reputation, its loyal customers, etc. Presumably, someone who spent this amount to create a similar hardware store would have to invest significant time to develop a comparable customer base.

Capitalization of Earnings

One of the more common, and relatively straightforward, methods of valuation is the capitalization of earnings method. Essentially, this method uses a risk rate to assess the value needed to generate the same amount of income as the business being valued.

Consider the following in the case of Cunningham Hardware. Suppose it is expected to generate exactly $10,000 each year in income indefinitely. So if the owner is trying to sell the store, the buyer would expect to receive this amount in annual income. Because the store is expected to generate this income level consistently, it should not lose its value. Now, if the buyer can earn a guaranteed rate of interest of 5% elsewhere, what amount of investment would be needed to generate $10,000 each year in income?

$$\text{Investment} \times 5\% = \$10,000$$
$$\$10,000/5\% = \$200,000$$

So an investment of $200,000 would earn $10,000 in interest each year, meaning the hardware store has a value of $200,000.

Unfortunately, such risk-free situations rarely exist. The owner of a hardware store undoubtedly assumes risks in day-to-day business dealings. So with increased risk, a higher capitalization rate would have to be assessed to estimate fair value. These rates will vary, and some might argue that they are entirely arbitrary. It is possible to use one of the cost of capital measures discussed in Chapter 7 or to consider rates used in comparable businesses. Regardless of the methodology, the result will prove highly sensitive to this rate. As such, many analysts believe the capitalization of earnings method is problematic.

Excess Earning Method

A variation on the capitalization of earnings method is the excess earning method. The major difference is that this method separates return on assets from the excess earnings. Supposing Cunningham Hardware has assets of $28,000 and earns $10,000 per year. Suppose the reasonable return on assets in this industry is 10%, which indicates expected earnings of $2,800 off assets ($28,000 × 10% = $2,800). The remaining $7,200 ($10,000 − $2,800 = $7,200) represents the excess earnings. This excess earnings number, in turn, is multiplied by a factor that incorporates risk, growth potential, and competitiveness. The factor is part estimation and part comparison. So if the factor in this case is 3, fair value is estimated to be $21,600 ($7,200 × 3 = $21,600). This type of methodology works for smaller companies with substantial tangible assets such as PP&E, inventory, receivables, and cash. Wall Street analysts tend to place little emphasis on this method, and so you probably just wasted your time learning it.

Discounted Cash Flow Valuation

The discounted cash flow (DCF) method of valuation is one of the most commonly used methods of valuation. Most investment bankers know this method better than they know their own spouses, which probably explains a lot. Normally, the mere utterance of the term *DCF* (the more insidious banker term) sends first-year financial analysts running for cover. A good DCF model can take several weeks to prepare, which in turn translates into many long nights spent at the office. The reason DCF models tend to be so complicated and so time intensive has little to do with the actual DCF calculations and much more to do with the research involved in creating projections. The reality is that a DCF model is far simpler than the investment banks would like you to believe.

In fact, the entire process can be condensed into four steps:

1. Calculate projections for future cash flows.
2. Calculate the cost of capital, or as it's referred to here, the *discount rate*.
3. Calculate the present value for each year's cash flow.
4. Finally, take the total of these present value cash flows.

Completing these four steps provides a very close estimate of the valuation for the company. The sum of these discounted cash flows is the company's valuation . . . well, almost.

Example.   Below are Cunningham Hardware's five-year cash flow projections. Note that step 1 above—*calculate projections for future cash flows*—has already been done. In looking at this company, notice that in year one it has cash flows of $25,000; in year two its cash flow projections are $23,000; in year three cash flow projections are $30,000; in year four they are $33,000; and in year five they are $45,000.

Cunningham Hardware Projections

Period	I	2	3	4	5
Year	2007	2008	2009	2010	2011
Cash flow	$25,000	$23,000	$30,000	$33,000	$45,000
Discount rate (WACC) = 9%					

These projections were given by the company. Of course, the company probably spent several weeks preparing them, because in any cash flow projection model there are a lot of assumptions and a lot of variables. In fact, the backup to this could be several hundred pages long. However, the primary concern here is the output, which is simply the cash flow projections themselves.

Start with these cash flow projections and work on your own to calculate the present value for each of the five years. Fire up that calculator, and compute the present values using the formula that is repeated below. Remember, r represents the discount rate of 9%, which was calculated using the weighted average cost of capital (WACC), and n is the period for which present value is being determined. No peeking!

$$PV = CF/(1 + r)^n$$

At this point, you have calculated the present values. Compare your answers with the solutions below. Now, depending on how you chose to round or how your calculator was set to round, you should have come up with something approximately equal to these numbers:

Cunningham Hardware Projections

Period	1	2	3	4	5
Year	2007	2008	2009	2010	2011
Cash flow	$25,000	$23,000	$30,000	$33,000	$45,000

Discount rate (WACC) = 9%

$$\frac{CF}{(1 + r)^n} = \frac{\$25,000}{(1 + 0.09)^1} + \frac{\$23,000}{(1 + 0.09)^2} + \frac{\$30,000}{(1 + 0.09)^3} + \frac{\$33,000}{(1 + 0.09)^4} + \frac{\$45,000}{(1 + 0.09)^5}$$

PV	=	$22,936	+	$19,359	+	$23,166	+	$23,378	+	$29,247

In the first year, take the cash flow of $25,000 and divide it by 1 plus the discount rate. The discount rate in this case is given at 9%. In year two, take $23,000 and divide it by 1 plus the discount rate raised to the second power. In year three, divide the cash flow of $30,000 by 1 plus the discount rate to the third power. In year four, take the cash flow payment of $33,000 and divide it by 1 plus the discount rate raised to the fourth power. Finally, in year five, take the cash flow of $45,000 divided by 1 plus the discount rate raised to the fifth power. In total, the present values of Cunningham's future cash flows approximately equal $118,085.

Is this the value of the company? You took present values for each of these five-year cash flows. Next, you summed these present values and came up with a number around $118,000. In certain instances, you might conclude your analysis at this point. Those instances occur when, at the end of five years, the company simply dissolves, meaning there is no residual value. More often than not, however, the company continues to operate long after those projections end.

How do analysts account for what happens after the projections end? They use what is called *terminal value*. Terminal value is a concept used to calculate the value of an asset that continues after the projections end, or into perpetuity. There are a number of ways of calculating terminal value. A simple way is to multiply the last year's cash flow by some industry average multiple. This amount is then added to the five-year discounted cash flows. This practice is based on loose estimates, and for that reason it is often perceived to lack credibility. A better method involves using the present value of a perpetuity. A perpetuity is an instrument that makes payments year after year without end. You can use the formula to calculate a perpetuity that assumes growth or a simpler formula to calculate one without growth. The two formulas are given below:

$$\text{Perpetuity without growth} = \text{CF}/r$$
$$\text{Perpetuity with growth} = \text{CF}/(r - g)$$

where

$$\text{CF} = \text{cash flow}$$
$$r = \text{discount rate}$$
$$g = \text{growth rate}$$

In this case, the next step is to go back to the company and ask for a year six cash flow estimate. Once that year six cash flow is obtained, assume it stays constant each year after that. Suppose that the company wants to assume a year six cash flow of $50,000; and each year after that, cash flows remain constant at $50,000. Apply that $50,000 to the perpetuity calculation, which is $50,000 divided by the discount rate of 9%. This results in a perpetuity value of $555,556. Is that the final value? Can this simply be added to the present value and proposed to a client? No. There's something very important missing here.

Think about this: Cunningham's perpetuity value is $555,556. The total of the first year's cash flows, or first five years of cash flows, is $118,000. What's missing here is the present value of that perpetuity, because that $555,556 is essentially treated as the value at the beginning of year six. When those cash flow payments after year five were projected, they were done so from year six. When a total value for all of them was calculated, the value at the beginning of year six was determined. What needs to be done next is a calculation of the value of that perpetuity in today's dollars by discounting it back five years using the present value formula. So the present value of that perpetuity should approximately equal $361,073.

Now the numbers are in place to finalize a value. As a last step, add the present value of perpetuity to the total discounted cash flows for the first five years, $118,085. That results in a company valuation of $479,158. At this point, the analysis on this company has concluded. A very detailed analysis has been formulated, one that can lend a great deal of credibility to the overall analysis of the company.

Comparable Multiple Valuation

The final method of valuation is the most commonly used and probably the easiest to use as well. For this reason, it is widely regarded as the quick and dirty method of valuation by Wall Street bankers. It is based on benchmarking one company against an industry-average multiple such as the price-to-earnings ratio. For example, an analyst will take the price of a company's stock and divide it by the company's earnings. This could also be applied to other variations on this multiple, such as price to EBIT or price to EBITDA. The following example keeps it simple and uses the basic price-to-earnings (P/E) ratio.

Generally speaking, if the company's price-to-earnings ratio is greater than the industry average, it is fair to say that the company is overvalued. If the company's P/E ratio is less than the industry average, it is fair to say that the company is undervalued. However, I always caution myself when I state this because, as is the case in most of finance and accounting, no rules are without exception. As you saw in Chapter 6 on financial analysis, many companies are seemingly undervalued, but for good reason. For example, a company might be a party in a pending lawsuit, and so the market has specifically undervalued the company because it is unclear what the ruling might be.

In instances like that, investors will not necessarily scramble to acquire shares of the company, even knowing that based on any type of valuation methodology, the company is undervalued.

Prices on a per-share basis

	Share Price	Earnings/Share	P/E
Beta Hardware	$36	$2	18
Gamma Hardware	$72	$3	24
Theta Hardware	$64	$4	16
Sigma Hardware	$36	$2	18
Industry average			19
Cunningham Hardware	?	$4	

By using the industry average P/E ratio, we calculate a fair value for Cunningham Hardware:

Industry P/E × company earnings = company fair value

19 × $4   = $76 per share

$76 × 1,600 shares   = $121,600

Figure 8.1   Comparable Multiple Evaluation

The comparable multiple method of valuation forms at least a starting point for making some basic assumptions about a company's value.

Take a look at the sample comparable multiple valuation model in Figure 8.1. The four companies listed constitute a sample peer group for which a price-to-earnings multiple will be calculated and applied to the target company (Cunningham Hardware). The first company has a share price of $36 per share. It has earnings per share of $2. So divide $36 per share by $2 earnings per share to come up with a P/E multiple of 18. The second company has a share price of $72 per share. It has earnings per share of $3. Divide that $72 by $3 to come up with a P/E multiple of 24. The third company has a share price of $64 per share and earnings per share of $4, which yields a P/E ratio of 16. Finally, the fourth company has a share price of $36 per share and earnings per share of $2, which yields a P/E ratio of 18.

To get the industry average, take a straight average of these four P/E ratios—18, 24, 16, and 18. Add them up, divide by 4, and the resulting industry average P/E is 19. Now it is possible to apply that industry average of 19 to the target company whose earnings are $4 per share. On the basis of this average, what do you think the share price or the perceived value of this company would be? If you calculated $76, you're absolutely right. This is calculated on a per-share basis; to find the value of the company, multiply the share price by the total number of shares outstanding. If it is assumed that the company has 1,600 shares outstanding, the total company market value is $121,600. That is the expected market capitalization, or the value of this company. This is the same company that was valued earlier using the discounted cash flow method that revealed a value of $479,000. So one method reveals a value of $479,000, whereas another reveals a value of $121,600. Is this a problem? Yes, indeed. If you are an analyst and this company is your client, you have a mild crisis when your two valuations do not coincide.

This reminds me of one of my first experiences in investment banking. Years ago, I received a call late one evening from a senior banker in my group. He began with, "Guess what? We just secured the right to represent a large corporation on a sell-side transaction. I need your team to help me produce a valuation for this company, and to do that, I'd like two valuation models. First, I'd like a discounted cash flow model and, second, a comparable multiple model. Oh, and whatever happens, I need you to make sure that the values on each come out to $100 million."

More often than not, investment bankers have their value in mind long before they plunge into the models. The goal with any financial model is to justify that value. Valuation models are simply mechanisms for engendering dialogue and building credibility. When using two valuation models, analysts often seek to ensure that these valuation models converge on the same number. In order to do that, they would come back to one of the two numbers, usually the lower of the two, $121,600 in the above example, and look at ways to increase it. Perhaps they might eliminate one of the multiples that bring the average down. The third company here has a relatively low P/E number. They might exclude that for one reason or another. They might look at a slightly different way of calculating P/E. Perhaps right now they are using projected earnings. They might instead use historic earnings that would potentially yield a higher industry average P/E. And through some clever adjustments, they might boost the industry average P/E ratio, which in turn would boost the expected share price, and in turn boost the company's valuation. In doing that, they would converge on that original discounted cash flow valuation number. Finally, they would have two different methods of analysis that reveal roughly the same number of valuation, and that is something they could bring to their client. Again, the only true value of a company is what the buyer and seller agree on.

> **Riddle:** What do you call a company with negative
> historic cash flows and positive projected cash flows?
> **Answer:** You call it an Internet company.

You cannot calculate a meaningful P/E ratio without positive earnings, and the market's failure to acknowledge this is essentially what drove the rise and subsequent fall of the Internet economy.

Net Present Value

A common measure often heard in the world of investment banking is net present value, or NPV. Investment bankers use this term quite frequently in their discussion with clients. For the most part, it is a useful concept. NPV is derived from basic principles of discounting future returns. If you recall, a company can be valued by forecasting future returns (cash flow, income, EBITDA, etc.) and discounting them based on some discount rate. From there, these present values of future returns can be summed and a fair value can be assessed for the company. Now what happens if the initial investment needed to launch that company is subtracted out? Net present value is left. Assume that $100,000 is needed to start the hardware store, which will generate present values of future cash flows that, in total, amount to $120,000. Once the initial investment is subtracted, $20,000 remains, the NPV.

NPV is calculated with the simple formula below:

$$NPV = \text{present value of future returns} - \text{investment}$$

When NPV is positive, the entrepreneur would probably move forward with the company. If NPV is negative, it would not make sense to move forward. Bankers like this measure because it reveals a return in cash and factors in risk based on a discount rate. Ultimately, bankers want to see that a deal makes money because they can always extract a fee from it. Investors such as venture capitalists, on the other hand, will tend to look at the internal rate of return, or IRR.

IRR, according to most textbooks, is the maximum rate of interest that could be paid for capital employed over the life of an investment in order for it to break even. This definition takes an already complicated concept and makes it more complicated. I prefer a more informal definition of IRR, which is the discount rate at which the sum of present values of future cash flows equals the initial investment. This is still a bit confusing, but take a look at the example in Figure 8.2.

Example: Cunningham Hardware Co.

	Investment	Projections				
Period	0	1	2	3	4	5
Year	2005	2006	2007	2008	2009	2010
Cash flow (CF)	$(118,085)	$25,000	$23,000	$30,000	$33,000	$45,000

$$\frac{CF}{(1+r)^n} = \frac{\$25,000}{(1+0.09)^1} + \frac{\$23,000}{(1+0.09)^2} + \frac{\$30,000}{(1+0.09)^3} + \frac{\$33,000}{(1+0.09)^4} + \frac{\$45,000}{(1+0.09)^5}$$

$$\$22,936 \quad \$19,359 \quad \$23,166 \quad \$23,378 \quad \$29,247$$

PV of cash flows = $118,085
Initial investment = $118,085
IRR = 9%

9% is the discount rate at which the present values of future cash flows equal the initial investment.

Figure 8.2   Internal Rate of Return

In this case, we projected future cash flows. Suppose the company dissolves at the end of year five and assume that the amount needed to get this company up and running is around $118,000. Based on this, the discount rate that would cause the present value of these future returns to equal the initial investment is 9%. It is the breakeven discount rate, or the IRR. IRR is useful in preference decisions. For example, a venture capitalist might review hundreds of proposals per month but may determine that only the ones with an IRR exceeding the firm's hurdle rate are worth investing in. If the firm has on average returned 20% per year, it is highly probable that the firm would designate this as its hurdle rate. So projects with an IRR greater than 20% would probably receive a closer look than ones with an IRR lower than 20%. Again, no decision should be based exclusively on IRR, or any other single performance measure for that matter,

Method	Accept	Reject	Indifferent
NPV	> 0	< 0	= 0
IRR	> *k*	< *k*	= *k*

Note: *k* denotes the required rate of return or cost of capital.

Figure 8.3   NPV versus IRR—Evaluating Projects

but the IRRs do provide a reasonable starting point. Before you go on to the next chapter, have a look at Figure 8.3. It offers a brief comparison of NPV and IRR in evaluating projects.

CHAPTER 9

Wall Street Basics: Stocks and Bonds

When I finished college, I was up to my ears in debt and somewhat envious of my former classmates who had their education paid for by their parents. My envy turned to sympathy when a friend explained to me that those who receive parental funding faced the burdens of managing their primary equity investors, namely, their parents. Their personal and professional pursuits would therefore be subject to the approval of their board of directors, composed exclusively of mom and dad. Those of us who went the debt route would be beholden only to our creditors, namely, the banks. The banks only demand repayment of principal in a timely manner, and other than that, they issue few demands. Therefore, we suffer no equity dilution and maintain complete voting power in all decisions. Of course, this sounded nice until I tried to exercise newly realized autonomy with a post-college European adventure only to learn the hard way that parents function more like a third-world dictatorship, where any business is subject to the whims of the government.

The balance sheet helps to understand the overall financial health of a company. A substantial portion of understanding the health is knowing what makes it tick, namely, the underlying capital structure. A question that arises in many discussions about the balance sheet is, "What is the best way to capitalize a company? Is it equity or debt?" The answer is, "It depends, as both debt and equity have their advantages."

Debt offers the following advantages. First, lenders have no direct claim on future earnings, and so debt can be issued without the worries of a claim on earnings. As long as the interest is paid, the company is fine. Second, the interest paid on debt can be deducted for tax purposes. Most payments, whether they are interest or principal payments, are usually predictable, and so a company can plan ahead and budget for them. Third, debt does not dilute the owner's interest, and so an owner can issue debt and not worry about a reduced equity stake. Finally, interest rates are usually lower than the expected return. If they are not, then a change in management can be expected soon.

Debt securities can take a number of different forms, the most common being bonds. Bonds are obligations secured by a mortgage on some company property. Bonds tend to be safer from the investor standpoint, and as such, they pay lower interest. Debentures, on the other hand, are unsecured and are issued on the strength of the company's reputation, projected earnings, or growth potential. Debentures, being far riskier, tend to pay more interest than their more secure counterparts.

Equity includes the following advantages. One, equity does not raise a company's breakeven point. So a company can issue equity and not have to worry about achieving performance benchmarks to fund the equity. Now, of course, any company that issues equity has to meet certain investor expectations, but the breakeven point of the company is not adjusted as a result of an equity issuance. Equity does not increase the risk of insolvency, and so a company can issue equity and not have to worry about any subsequent payments to service that equity. Equity is essentially capital with unlimited life, and so a company can issue equity and not have to worry about a time when it comes due.

Finally, there is no need to pledge assets or offer any personal guarantees when equity is issued.

Equity can take on a number of different forms. A simple form of equity is common stock. Common stock offers no limits on the rate of return and can continue to rise in price indefinitely. There are no fixed terms; the stock is simply issued, and the holder bears the stock. Preferred stock entitles the holders to receive dividends at a fixed or adjustable rate of return and ranks higher than common stock in a liquidation. In fact, preferred stock may have antidilution rights, so that in a subsequent stock offering, preferred stockholders may maintain the same equity stake. Nowadays, we're seeing the issuance of more and more convertible securities. These securities are highly structured in nature and based on certain parameters; and as the word *convertible* indicates, they may convert into other securities. Among the most common are warrants and options. Warrants and options stand for the right to buy a stated number of shares of common or preferred stock at a specified time for a specified price. There are also convertible notes and preferred stock, which refer to the right to convert these notes to some common stock when the conversion price is more favorable than the current rate of return.

These highly structured securities can be very problematic. It reminds me of a story about a transaction I worked on years ago during my days on Wall Street. At the time, we came up with a clever offering for a large oil company. The offering was structured around a form of preferred stock that could be called by the company at any time and that at maturity had to be redeemed into either cash or common shares. The entire offering was predicated on very detailed statistical analysis—the kind that even the most sophisticated fund managers had difficulty grasping. When the offering was marketed to the large fund managers, most of them left the room entirely perplexed. As a result, the offering wasn't nearly as successful as the investment bankers had hoped. Needless to say, our closing dinner was canceled and the deal was never mentioned again.

In this chapter, we will discuss the following:

- Bonds
- Stocks

Bonds

So much of Wall Street, and the U.S. economy as a whole, is driven by the debt markets. When the Fed raises interest rates, it affects every one of us in some form. The strategies that corporations employ to manage their debt can drive the company's overall performance. Bonds, or what are generally referred to as *secured debts*, have a number of distinguishing features. Here is a brief explanation of each:

- *Amount (of issue)*. How much was raised from the offering
- *Date (of issue)*. The day of sale
- *Maturity*. When the principal will be repaid
- *Face value*. Denomination of the bond
- *Offer price*. The percentage of the face value
- *Coupon*. The percentage of interest paid to bondholders (usually stated in annual terms)
- *Coupon payment dates*. Dates of interest payments
- *Call provision*. Does the company retain the right to repay the bond prior to maturity
- *Call price*. If there is a call provision, the price at which the company can buy the bond back (usually above the bond's value, thus offering some premium for early repayment)

Types of Bonds: Corporate and Government

Among the broader classifications of bonds are corporate and government, with payment structures of zero coupon, fixed rate, and floating rate. Of course, there are variations on these and numerous exotic bonds, but these classifications generally encompass the extensive universe of bonds.

Corporate bonds.   Corporate bonds can take many forms, but for the most part, an issuance of long-term debt to the public by a company is considered a corporate bond offering. A corporate bond will list most, if not all, of the features above in its prospectus and will be traded in the open market, both on and off the major exchanges. Most of these bonds will be rated by one of the major rating agencies such as Standard & Poor's or Moody's. These ratings will be based on the creditworthiness of the issuer, which will factor a number of variables used to determine the probability of default. The higher the likelihood of default, the lower the rating. The bond prices, as you will see later, are highly sensitive to these ratings. However, the prices will also be sensitive to changes in interest rates, although these will not be factored into the ratings. The ratings will range from AAA (S&P) and Aaa (Moody's) to D (S&P) and C (Moody's). A bond's ratings will affect its pricing. When a company falls to a rating of BB (S&P) or Ba (Moody's), it is called *junk* (also know as *high yield* in more refined circles), meaning it is highly speculative and prone to risk of default.

Government bonds.   Most countries across the globe will finance a portion of their activities through the issuance of bonds. In many of these countries though, payback will never happen. However, the United States has a pretty good track record with this. In fact, the largest debtor in the world is the

U.S. government, so we should all hope that this trend continues. The U.S. government issues Treasury bills, notes, and bonds to finance its activities, with maturities on the latter two ranging from 2 to 30 years. Treasuries are considered risk-free (at least for now) and are state tax exempt. Most of these are simple coupon bonds.

Like the federal government, state and local governments will issue municipal (muni) bonds. These can have higher levels of risk and are often related to a specific project, such as the construction of a dam. Furthermore, they are usually callable. The most appealing quality of these bonds to the investor is the fact that they are federal tax exempt. Due to the tax benefit of these bonds, their yields tend to be significantly lower than those of corporate bonds. Nonetheless, munis provide a compelling investment option for investors in the highest tax bracket.

Consider the following: You decide to invest in one of two bonds. One, a corporate bond, pays 7% and is taxable, while the other, a muni, pays 5% and is federal tax exempt. If you are in a 40% tax bracket, which would you choose?

On the taxable corporate bond, after tax you would earn $7\% \times (1 - 40\%) = 4.2\%$. On the tax-exempt muni, you would earn 5%.

Types of Bonds: Zero Coupon, Fixed Rate, and Floating Rate

Zero coupon bonds. Zero coupon bonds are priced at a discount to par, with the difference accounting for the interest that would be paid. For example, a five-year, zero coupon bond priced at $750 would pay $250 in interest ($1,000 − $750 = $250). The $250 accounts for the difference between the $1,000 par value and the initial price. Presumably, one-fifth of that $250, or $50, would count as interest for each year. In some cases, these bonds pay no coupons for a period of time and then commence coupon payments, thus functioning as a type of convertible instrument.

Fixed- and floating-rate bonds.   Aside from the zero coupon bonds, most bonds will make some sort of coupon or interest payment. Fixed-rate bonds will make a payment based on a fixed rate of interest. If that rate is 5%, then a $1,000 bond will pay $50 per year. Floating-rate bonds, by contrast, will make payments based on some variable rate of interest that is usually tied to an interest index such as Treasury rates or LIBOR (London Interbank Offering Rate). These indexes adjust periodically based on various economic factors, as well as those influenced by governmental monetary policy. When they adjust, so do the floating-rate coupons.

Bond Pricing and Valuation

Now comes the tricky part—bond pricing. Below is a bond quote for the company Car-E-Oki, as it would appear in the newspaper:

Bond	Current Yield	Close	Change
CEO 8 1/2 10	8.6	98.35	−0.42

This bond pays 8.5% of its face value in interest and matures in 2010. With a face value of $1,000, the bond would pay $85 in interest per year. This bond closed at 98.35, or 98.35% of its face value of $1,000, which would be $983.50. The closing price dropped 0.42%, or $4.20, since yesterday's close. The current yield, probably the most important component of the quote, shows what would be earned based on the current price and coupon. Divide the coupon by the closing price to calculate this (8.5%/98.35% = 8.6%). Additional information, such as volume numbers, might show up in a more detailed quote.

What drives that bond price and, correspondingly, the yield? In other words, how are these bonds valued? A number of factors influence this. Among them are:

- Interest rates
- Inflation
- Credit risk
- Liquidity

Inflation and interest tend to work in tandem. If the outlook of high inflation is prevalent, interest rates will increase to compensate for this. Credit risk has to do with the creditworthiness of the company. In the case of Treasuries, this would not factor in because Treasuries are considered to be risk-free. Liquidity will influence prices, as investors typically prefer more liquid assets over less liquid ones. Therefore, some liquidity premium will have to be offered to entice investors when a bond is less liquid.

Junk Bonds

A long time ago in a city far, far away (Beverly Hills), there came a time of revolution when corporate America fell prey to bold promises and great parties. During this time, corporations raised billions of dollars, while corporate managers, investment bankers, and traders bilked the public out of billions of dollars. They did so through the skillful use of junk bonds.

Junk bonds grew in popularity as corporations experienced a drop in credit quality resulting from a change in business or financing conditions. As more statisticians and financial analysts began to study the returns on junk bond portfolios, they soon determined that the risk-adjusted returns on a portfolio of junk bonds were higher than the risk assumed. Pioneers in this market, such as Michael Milken and his firm, Drexel Burnham Lambert, were successful in perpetuating this theory, which led to billions of dollars in fees for the underwriters, and according to many, helped fuel the explosive economic growth of the 1980s. For the first time, large amounts of capital were made available to risky ventures, which resulted in the expansion of industries such as cable television, telecommunications, and home building. Although Milken was not the originator of the junk bond, he is credited with bringing these bonds to the masses. Through his massive network of money managers, he was able to place these bonds with funds all over the United States.

Milken's early career was marked by long hours in Drexel's bond group, working on "fallen angels," bonds of once great corporations that had been downgraded to junk by the rating agencies. His role was to determine whether the risk of default was outweighed by the interest premium paid. What Milken discovered was revolutionary. Milken's challenge to convention began with the rating agencies. He saw that the rating agencies offered investment-grade ratings to the top several hundred corporations in America. These were established companies with large market capitalizations and proven performance. However, tens of thousands of other corporations were excluded from traditional Wall Street debt underwriting due to their limited size and histories. Such companies could only borrow from commercial lenders or insurance companies at unpredictable short-term rates and under restrictive covenants.

Milken felt this system was inherently flawed because top-rated companies could easily see a drop in their bond prices due to a bankruptcy or industry slowdown, leading to credit downgrades. Based on this, he felt that the rating agencies focused too much on the past, namely the balance sheet, and not nearly enough on the future, namely cash flows. Milken initiated this new paradigm that linked bonds to future cash flows. Soon, he was underwriting debt that behaved more like equity. Not long after, corporate raiders and leverage buyout kings such as Ron Perlman, T. Boone Pickens, and Henry Kravis were lining up to secure funding through Milken.

Milken became a buyer, seller, market maker, and underwriter of these bonds, the combination of which probably led to his undoing. By assuming that much control over a single market, he raised scrutiny on his activities to a new level. The fact that he was making over half a billion dollars per year did not help matters either. Eventually, an insider trading scandal brought down Drexel Burnham and put Mr. Milken in jail.

Stocks

Just as important as bond valuation is stock valuation. The interesting thing about stocks is that even with detailed formulas and models, you might just think you have it all figured out. However, we will soon see that none of this really matters, because the markets are inherently irrational.

Despite all the emphasis placed on valuing common stock, ultimately the process of valuation is wrought with uncertainty and controversy. For example, little is known regarding a company's future cash flows; and more importantly, a stock does not have a maturity date like a bond, and so its life is forever. Nonetheless, equity research analysts, fund managers, and speculators devote most of their waking hours to this practice. Take a look at how stocks are valued based on some of the valuation principles that have already been covered.

Discounted Cash Flows

As shown in Chapter 8 on valuation, the value of a company can be assessed based on the sum of the present value of future cash flows. So an equity analyst will build out these detailed cash flow models, come up with a discount rate, take the present value of these projected cash flows, and add them all up. The final step, barring any adjustments, would be to divide the company value by the number of shares outstanding to determine a value on a per-share basis. This would form the basis of the price target assessed by the analyst.

Dividend Method

Another method of assessing stock values is to project a stream of dividends and discount them to present value. The idea is that dividends represent the return on a stock. So these dividends can be treated the same way projected cash flows would be treated. If the dividend is assumed to grow at a constant rate, the stock price would be modeled as follows:

$$P = D_1/(1 + r)^1 + D_2/(1 + r)^2 + D_3/(1 + r)^3 + D_4/(1 + r)^4 \\ + D_5/(1 + r)^5 + D_6/(1 + r)^6 + D_7/(1 + r)^7 \ldots$$

In theory, the sum of the present values would yield a stock price. But where does it all end? Do these dividend projections stop? How can the dividend be forecasted for each future year? Why am I even doing this?

Attempting to answer these questions would just further complicate matters. However, that has never stopped us before. So, in theory, the stream of dividends does not end. In this case, a perpetuity value would be assigned to one of the projected dividends and discounted back to present value. Again, the same principles used in discounted cash flow valuation are applied.

As far as forecasting the dividend goes, there are a number of ways to do this. The simplest, of course, is to assume it does not change. In that case, a simple perpetuity calculation could be used, which would look something like this:

$$P = D/r$$

Also, assume that the dividend grows at a constant rate using the formula for a perpetuity with growth. In this case, a dividend would be used instead of a cash flow:

$$P = D/(r - g)$$

So there you have it. The value of a stock is the sum of the present values of future dividends. What happens, though, when a company does not pay dividends? Then you're back to good old-fashioned comparables. As seen in Chapter 8 on valuation, companies are often valued relative to industry-average multiples, such as the price-to-earnings ratio. In fact, most publicly traded companies are valued this way. What happens if there are few comparables to value a company against? Well, then you're on your own. I suggest you read a real finance book such as Brealey and Myers's *Principles of Corporate Finance* and get back to me when you've done so. I'd love to hear what they have to say.

CHAPTER 10

Wall Street Part Deux: Arbitrage, Derivatives, and Hedge Funds

Years ago, a colleague of mine and I would frequent a local Indian restaurant near our office in Manhattan. As each of us was on a fairly tight budget, we applied our skills in finance to optimize our food consumption while minimizing our cost. The chicken tikka plate, which came with six pieces of chicken and a bowl of rice, was priced at $11.95. The chicken tikka appetizer, which came with three pieces of chicken, was priced at $3.95. A bowl of rice was $1.95. What do you think we did? As pioneers in the chicken tikka arbitrage market, we figured that by ordering off the appetizer menu, we were able to consume six pieces of chicken and a bowl of rice for $9.85, saving $2.10 from the dinner menu. In fact, had we been more sophisticated arbitrageurs, we might have considered selling our meal to the table next to us for $10.95, earning us just over a dollar and saving the table a dollar. However, I'm sure that had we done this, the market would have corrected and we would have been shown the door.

In this chapter, we will discuss the following:

- Arbitrage
- Derivatives
- Forwards

- Futures
- Orange County
- Hedge funds

Arbitrage

Arbitrage, technically speaking, is the simultaneous purchase and sale of an asset or security to capitalize on price differentials that might exist between different marketplaces or exchanges. In other words, it is an opportunity to earn a return on a transaction without assuming any risk. For example, suppose the spot price for gold in the United States is $400 per ounce. In the United Kingdom, it should trade at the same price. However, because of fluctuations in the currency exchange rate, at this very moment it is selling for $401 per ounce. With some sophisticated software and rapid-fire decision-making skills, the gold can be purchased in the United States and, within a second, sold in the United Kingdom for a $1 profit, representing the momentary difference. Granted, the return is only 0.25%, but a big player in this market might have just made a $100 million trade leading to a $250,000 profit for a second of work. Not bad.

Obviously, such trades are few and far between; and they are rarely this simple. Moreover, a number of costs were incurred in the process of finding such a trade. It is quite likely that such a trade occurs only once every few years. Of the other such trades that were attempted, most ended up losing when the market corrected at the time of sale. So a person may try several trades but only see a return on one. Plus, there is always the risk that the price may fall when selling, causing a monetary loss. This type of arbitrage is risky, and the process of finding such opportunities can be time consuming.

Currency Arbitrage

Currency arbitrage is one of the most profitable forms of arbitrage. Suppose that the exchange rate between British pounds (GBP) and U.S. dollars (USD) is 2. So one could trade £5 for $10. The USD-to-GBP rate would, in turn, be 0.5. However, what happens if the USD-to-GBP market is 0.6 for a moment? One could then trade $10 for £6. In this process, £1 is earned. In theory, the market will soon correct, but for a fleeting moment, a class of arbitrageurs has done its best to exploit this difference.

A more complex form of such a trade is one in which three currencies are traded simultaneously. For example, suppose GBP to USD is 2 and USD to Canadian dollars (CAD) is 3. To figure out the appropriate exchange rate of GBP to CAD, multiply:

$$GBP \text{ to } CAD = (GBP \text{ to } USD) \times (USD \text{ to } CAD)$$

The rate would be 6, and likewise, the CAD to GBP would be 1/6. What happens, however, if it is 1/5 for a brief moment? Again, there is an arbitrage opportunity. One could take £5, swap them for $10 US, and then take the $10 US and exchange them for $30 Canadian. Finally, if the CAD-to-GBP rate is 1/5, one could now trade the $30 Canadian for £6. In aggregate, one extra British pound was earned.

In many cases of arbitrage, hefty transaction costs preclude traders from executing the transaction. As a result, currency arbitrage tends to be more common than other types, due to the lower transaction costs. Some other types of arbitrage are detailed below.

Merger Arbitrage

Merger arbitrage is the simultaneous purchase and sale of two companies involved in a proposed merger. A merger arbitrageur analyzes the probability of the merger not closing within the stated time frame or at all. Because of this uncertainty, the target company's stock price trades at a slight discount to the acquirer's offer price. So the merger arbitrageur might assess a high probability that the deal will close, and as such, profit from the price differential. Remember a guy named Ivan Boesky? He helped make merger arbitrage part of mainstream finance vernacular. In the mid-1980s, Boesky amassed a fortune of some $200 million and established himself as one of the best arbitrageurs the world had known. What investors and regulators failed to see for quite some time was that his massive stock purchases occurred only days before a corporation announced a takeover. Boesky was relying on tips from his pal Michael Milken and using the information to make lucrative stock trades. Boesky became an icon of Wall Street bravado, going so far as to tell a room full of college students in 1986, "I think greed is healthy. You can be greedy and still feel good about yourself," a line that inspired Michael Douglas's speech in the movie *Wall Street*. Eventually, SEC investigators got wind of Mr. Boesky's dealings and sent him to prison for two years.

Index Arbitrage

Sometimes stock traders will find minor discrepancies in the pricing of index funds and the individual stocks that compose them. In such instances, traders might buy the index and simultaneously short the individual stocks. These trades tend to be more complex and often involve dealing with several dozen or more individual stocks.

Convertible-Debt Arbitrage

With these instruments, you might have the option to convert your debt to common stock at a certain price. In rare instances, you might be able to convert at one price and then sell at a different market price.

Barings Bank

One of the greatest tales of arbitrage gone awry deals with Barings Bank. Barings had a long history as one of the most respected banks in the United Kingdom. In early 1995, the bank was bankrupted by $1 billion in trading losses attributed to one trader by the name of Nick Leeson. Leeson, who made a name for himself on Wall Street, was appointed as general manager of Barings Futures in Singapore. In this position, he had responsibilities in both trading and administration, which created an opportunity for him to hide unauthorized trading activities. Over the next several years, Leeson took sizable positions in an effort to capitalize on arbitrage opportunities between the Singapore International Monetary Exchange (Simex) and the Osaka Exchange. However, the senior managers at Barings, who were merchant bankers and not seasoned traders, believed that these were evenly matched positions. The positions were assumed to be low-risk, low-profit positions. In reality, Leeson was trading derivatives on the two exchanges that in some cases were mismatched in size. For example, he would create a straddle (simultaneously selling a put and a call) with the hope that the markets would remain relatively flat. If this happened, the options would expire, and he would have profited from the premiums received through their sale. If the markets were volatile, such positions could result in large losses.

Leeson maintained an error account to conceal his losses. He hoped that through subsequent gains, these losses would be wiped out and the account reduced to a zero balance. As losses mounted, he took on larger positions with the hope of recouping these losses sooner rather than later. The need to emerge from this hole fueled his intensity to take risks and disguise losses. Leeson's story unraveled when the Nikkei 225 fell 1,000 points after a major earthquake hit Japan in early 1995. This unforeseen occurrence caused Leeson to suffer inordinate losses and raised questions surrounding the legitimacy of his accounts. Two months later, Barings, unable to craft a realistic plan to emerge from financial catastrophe, was sold to the Dutch bank ING for 1 pound sterling. Thus, the tale of this once prestigious European boutique that helped the United States finance the Louisiana Purchase over a century earlier came to an end.

Derivatives

I once knew a young woman who dated unemployed men with multiple degrees from prestigious schools. I respected the fact that she was drawn to their intellect, but never quite understood the appeal of unemployment. In fact, most of them lived with their mothers and spent the majority of their days playing online games or watching the sci-fi channel. I one day mustered up the courage to discuss this somewhat unconventional practice with her and asked, "Why are you consistently attracted to this type of guy?" She readily responded, "Some people buy the overpriced stock; I buy the call option. You see, these guys do not demand much up front, show a lot of promise, and may some day be worth quite a bit. So if even one makes it big, I'm set. I've created a risk-weighted portfolio of call options."

Sadly, she was hoping one of these guys would become the next Bill Gates, but like many of the high-risk tech companies in the late nineties . . . well, let's just say they still live with mommy and the options expired.

Derivative securities are securities based on the movement of some underlying security or index. This might include stocks, bonds, commodities, currencies, or even indexes. Derivatives were originally created to hedge against market risk, and today there is an abundance of such instruments, although the more common ones include options, warrants, and swaps.

Options

An ordinary option grants the holder the right to buy or sell something at a specified price within a specified period of time. The most basic forms of options are calls and puts.

Call options. With a call, the option holder is able to purchase a security (for example, a stock) at a certain price. Suppose you have your eye on that company that just invented Car-E-Oki—the karaoke machine for the car. The company, which trades under the ticker CEO, is offered at $10 per share. You have $1,000 to invest, which would get you 100 shares of CEO. CEO is about to announce the release of its new machine, made exclusively for pickup trucks. Now everyone will be able to enjoy live country music on America's highways, something you believe will cause the stock to appreciate nicely. So if you buy 100 shares of CEO and the stock doubles this year, you will have made $1,000. Not a bad return.

However, you are extremely confident that the stock will double, and as such, you are seeking to maximize the highest returns possible with your investment. Rather than buy the stock, you buy the call option. The call option gives you the right to buy the stock at a specific price within a fixed period of time. In this case, the January 10 call options trade at $1. So you could buy the right to purchase one share of stock before next January at the price of $10 per share. In fact, with $1,000, you could buy the right to purchase 1,000 shares. Assuming you do this and the stock price doubles between now and next January, how much have you made?

You bought 1,000 options, each representing the right to buy one share. If you were to exercise these options, meaning purchase the shares at the strike price of $10, you would own $10,000 worth of the stock. If the stock goes to $20 per share, effectively doubling in value, your position would now be worth $20,000. In total, you would recognize a gain of $10,000, less the $1,000 to purchase the options initially, for a net gain of $9,000. This is considerably more than the $1,000 you would have made simply buying 100 shares of stock in the first place. What happens if you do not have the funds to purchase those 1,000 shares of stock? No problem. Prior to the expiration date, you need not exercise the option. Rather, the option will appreciate in value as the stock price appreciates. With a $1,000 investment, you have net $9,000. Not bad. But if the stock price falls below $10, you lose your entire investment.

Put options. Consider another scenario. Suppose you are not willing to lose your $1,000 investment if you buy the call options and the stock drops below $10 at the time of expiration. Furthermore, you are interested in protecting your investment, or in other words, purchasing some sort of insurance on it. In this case, you might consider buying the stock outright and then purchasing put options to hedge against any drop in price. You might now purchase 100 shares at $10 each for a total of $1,000. You might also purchase January 10 puts at a price of $1. With these, you have the right to sell your shares at $10 even if the price falls below $10. In total, it costs you $100 for this right. If the stock goes up, you lose the full $100 that you spent on the puts. Hopefully though, the stock will appreciate more than that $1, providing you with some profit. Should the stock fall, the most you will lose is $1 per share. So $1 per option, or a total of $100, buys some insurance.

Put options can be pricey. You will see how these are valued next. Giving up 10% of your stock value can be considerable, especially when few stocks earn more than this. Furthermore, the stock price might remain flat throughout the life of the option and then fall after the option expires. Not only did you lose the option premium, but you are now left exposed to the drop. Buying longer-dated options, though, is more expensive.

Option valuation.   Option valuation is a tricky business. There are a number of ways to value these options, but consistently, most option models factor in the following:

- Strike price
- Expected option life
- Current stock price
- Expected dividends
- Volatility
- Risk-free rate

The most commonly used method is the Black-Scholes model. Back in the early 1970s, two guys by the names of Fisher Black and Myron Scholes wrote a paper in which they detailed a mathematical model used to value options. The model incorporates each of the above-mentioned factors and, through some sophisticated mathematical maneuvering, generates a number reflective of an option's fair value. The model is so widely used that most option traders regard this as the most important tool of the trade. At the same time, the Black-Scholes model is often criticized for a number of shortcomings. First, the model is driven heavily by historic movements of a stock, which may not accurately depict expected future developments. Second, the model is mathematically complex, and aside from the occasional Ph.D. in finance, few are comfortable using it. Finally, long-term, nontraded stock options would have little use for such a model.

Although alternatives to Black-Scholes exist, most financial managers prefer this method. The binomial lattice model (also known as *Cox, Ross, Rubenstein*) uses more inputs and is thus seen as more accurate. Nonetheless, Black-Scholes remains the preferred method due to its long history and, more than anything else, the concern over changing internal controls. Most CFOs would be reluctant to adopt a new standard, given the time and cost associated with development and training.

Option Arbitrage

As we saw earlier, arbitrage can be an effective way to profit from pricing discrepancies. Sometimes, options create such opportunities. Suppose you notice that Company ABC is trading at $50 per share. The call option to buy one share of ABC at $30 is trading at $10. You can buy the option for $10, exercise the call for $30, and sell the stock that you now own for $50. You have paid $10 for the option plus $30 for the stock for a total cost of $40. So you walk away with a $10 return. Such instances are extremely rare, although it is possible for an active options trader to pick up a discrepancy of a few basis points on a similar trade. If you are trading millions of dollars, this can amount to a nice return.

Warrants

Warrants are similar to options, with the largest differences stemming from duration. Aside from that, the differences are minor, as you can see in the table that follows:

Warrants	*Options*
Usually dated between three and five years	Usually dated less than nine months
Involves new shares being issued	No new shares issued
Issued by companies for investors	Contracts between investors
Traded on the stock exchange	Traded on an options exchange

Swaps

Swaps are a type of derivative in which two parties enter into an agreement to exchange their streams of cash flows. One of the more common types of these is interest rate swaps. Often, a company that pays a fixed rate of interest on corporate debt seeks to protect these payments from a fall in interest rates. These simple swaps are known as *vanilla interest swaps*. Typically, such an arrangement will involve two loans of the same denomination that pay interest on the same dates. One loan pays a fixed rate, and the other, a floating rate. Let's go back to the CEO example. Suppose you were just named CEO of CEO, or better yet, CFO of CEO. Your first order of business is to protect that new corporate debt issuance. The company issued $100 of corporate debt that pays 5% interest annually. Now, suppose you would prefer to service that debt using a floating rate. You could swap your fixed payments into floating payments. The difference between the two rates would be paid to you or paid out by you, depending on the fluctuations of the floating rate. Figure 10.1 depicts this.

Normally, vanilla interest rate swaps are quoted based on the fixed rate. So the difference between the fixed rate and the corresponding floating rate (U.S. Treasuries, LIBOR) would be

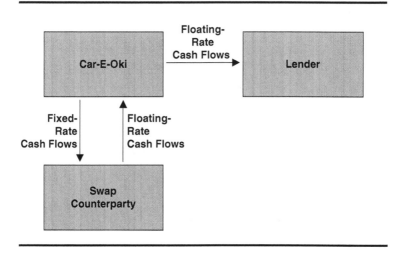

Figure 10.1 Swap Structures

quoted as the swap rate. Swaps are used not only by financial managers, but by bond traders as well. A trader betting on a rise in interest rates might enter into a pay-fixed swap.

Forwards

A forward contract is an obligation to transfer an asset at a specific price on a specific date. It is an effective hedge, especially in the commodities markets, which can be quite volatile and subject to forces outside of the market. The party that will sell the asset is called the *short* party, and the party that buys it is called the *long* party. When the deal is structured, no funds actually change hands.

One thing about the Car-E-Oki machine that was not mentioned earlier is its innovative design. The speaker box has a silver lining that further amplifies high-pitched singing. In fact, most of the cost of production is tied to this silver component. You recently received a large order from one of the major automakers to outfit all its new cars with Car-E-Oki machines. Production begins in about a month, and for that reason, you will need to oversee the purchase of materials. One of your biggest concerns right now is the price of silver, as that will constitute a large portion of your cost. You approach your supplier of silver and mention that you need a large delivery in one month. You are concerned that silver prices are rising and want to lock in a price today. To do that, you enter into a forward contract with the supplier.

One month has passed, and you take delivery of the silver at the price that was agreed upon. At this time, the current (spot) price of silver has increased considerably. You still pay the price agreed upon from the forward contract and breathe a sigh of relief for entering into it in the first place. Your supplier is clearly disappointed, knowing that he lost out on substantial gains. Nonetheless, he entered into the agreement initially to lock in place the sale. For him, it was a way to protect the sale. So, in the end, you got a fair price for the silver and your supplier got to lock in a sale. Both sides were able to effectively manage risk.

Futures

Futures are contracts to buy or sell an underlying asset on a particular date. Futures are generally traded over commodities such as oil, gold, wool, and frozen concentrated orange juice. When one buys a future contract, she is agreeing to buy a certain commodity or index on a certain date; and when one sells a future contract, she agrees to sell the underlying commodity or index on a certain date. The cash settlement that occurs on that date is based on the movement in price of the underlying commodity or index.

Futures can be used to:

- Hedge a portfolio position to protect it in the event of a market downturn.
- Achieve leveraged returns with a small investment, potentially leading to sizable returns.
- Capitalize on market declines; if the market should turn south, an investment could be protected and recognize sizable gains through the use of futures.

Futures and Valuation

Futures are valued based on market demand rather than a fixed or predetermined price. Futures traders will do their best to assess a fair value based on a calculation that is loosely equal to the underlying asset plus a premium, referred to as the *cost of carry*. The cost of carry pertains to any expenses incurred while holding that position. Consider the following example:

- The NASDAQ is currently at 2,000.
- Interest rates are at 4%.
- There are 180 days until maturity for this futures contract.
- Average dividend yield on stocks in this index is 2%.

To calculate the fair value, use the following formula:

Fair value = current level of NASDAQ + cost of carry
= 2,000 + [2,000 × (4% − 2%) × 180/365]
= 2,019.73

Like options, this premium will decrease as the maturity date approaches.

Orange County

Before Orange County, California, was know for its ability to churn quality television story lines, it was a hotbed of financial mismanagement. In the mid-1990s, the treasurer of Orange County made a bet that interest rates would remain low. He was not alone in this thinking, as many economic experts at the time held the same view. Unfortunately, the move cost the county $1.6 billion.

At the time, Robert Citron was among the most respected county treasurers in the country. Overseeing a pool of funds in excess of $7 billion, he crafted a strategy to invest these funds in a leveraged portfolio that primarily comprised interest-based securities. The strategy was predicated on the expectation that short-term interest rates would remain low, relative to medium-term rates. As the Fed began a strategy of raising rates, the OC portfolio began to lose value. By the end of 1994, mounting demands from government investors and Wall Street bankers created an insurmountable liquidity crunch for Mr. Citron. Eventually, the investors reached a settlement in bankruptcy court, receiving $0.77 per $1.00 invested, and Mr. Citron was sentenced to one year under house arrest plus a $100,000 fine. Meanwhile, the firm most responsible for advising Citron, Merrill Lynch, reached a $400 million settlement with Orange County in 1998, amid allegations that it had provided poor advice.

What happened? Ultimately, Citron used the following techniques to leverage a $7.5 billion fund into $20 billion in assets:

- *Reverse repurchase agreements.* By using securities already in the pool as collateral, he was able to further leverage his position. However, if the market value of these securities fell, they exposed him to margin calls.

- *Structured notes.* These derivatives included inverse floaters, index-amortizing notes, and collateralized mortgage obligations. Such instruments were highly structured and easily veiled in the reporting process, proving difficult for experts and analysts to discern the holdings in these structures.

All was fine provided short-term interest rates remained low, as was the case during the early 1990s. However, in February 1994, the Fed began a series of rate hikes that in total amounted to more than a 2% increase in rates by the end of 1994. Such a movement can be catastrophic to a multibillion dollar fund, especially one that is highly leveraged and invested in highly sensitive derivatives.

Hedge Funds

With exotic securities and innovative investing strategies on the rise, hedge funds are a popular means of achieving strong returns for high-net-worth individuals. These funds are formed through a managed portfolio that takes aggressive positions in what can often be highly speculative opportunities. Most of these funds are limited to a small pool of individual investors usually consisting of no more than 100. Hedge funds are generally unregulated, because it is assumed that the people investing in them are sophisticated investors. Investing strategies might involve derivatives, swaps, arbitrage, leverage, and short selling (selling a security that you don't own and then hopefully buying it at a lower price to fulfill the order and earn a nice profit). The problem is, however, that hedge funds do little in terms of hedging. In fact, they often take exceptionally large amounts of risk in an effort to produce astronomical returns. Most hedge fund managers will probably argue that they diversify against stock market risk by taking on complex positions. Whether or not this is true is a great source of debate. Nonetheless, hedge fund returns can be impressive, but once in a while, the results are disastrous.

CHAPTER 11

Mergers and Acquisitions

My first foray into the world of mergers and acquisitions (M&A) began years ago when I crafted a merger scenario between two major oil companies. It was a hypothetical scenario, but one that nonetheless revealed tremendous potential. In my analysis, I assumed cost savings by eliminating certain operating expenses, bringing about regional diversification (one company had major holdings in Colorado, the other in Texas), and creating production efficiencies resulting from better supply chain management. Despite these foreseeable benefits, I concluded that the merger would not work due to invariable management conflicts. The Ewings and the Carringtons would never get along.

M&A continues to be a driving force behind the global economy. Corporations seeking to fuel growth, boost profits, and increase shareholder value are constantly on the lookout for merger opportunities. Despite the flurry of multibillion dollar mergers that dominate business headlines these days, we still face the reality that many of these mergers fail to return what was promised to investors. To better understand why this occurs, we will examine the reasons for mergers along with some well-known cases in history. In this chapter, we will discuss the following:

History of M&A

The first major corporate mergers took place in the early nineteenth century when a trend of consolidation swept the railroad industry. Within a few years, the merger wave began in earnest, as William Procter and James Gamble merged their candle and soap companies. The second half of the nineteenth century was characterized by several noteworthy M&A trends, including the Singer Company's "role-up" of the sewing machine industry, as it sought to buy out most of its competitors. General Mills was formed through the consolidation of several milling companies, and General Electric was created through a merger between Edison General Electric and Thomson-Houston Electric. This early merger wave was without boundaries, and as such, concerns arose regarding the power these corporations wielded over the consumer. Eventually, the merger trend led to trusts, whereby equity holders placed the voting rights of their shares in the hands of a small committee of administrators. Trusts were formed in the steel, tobacco, sugar, and copper industries. They soon morphed into monopolies, which were eventually dismantled by the trust-buster himself, President Theodore Roosevelt.

The boom years of the 1920s brought about numerous mergers aimed at vertical integration. From the Depression through the decade following World War II, M&A activity was relatively quiet. In the 1960s, however, merger mania revived when stock swaps became an easy source of funding. By the 1980s, high-yield debt and easy access to it became a driving force behind large corporate mergers. This was followed by globalization and a booming stock market working in tandem to propel mergers in the 1990s. The new millennium has brought forth mergers between some of the world's largest corporations, with each new announcement eclipsing the last.

Types of Mergers

Generally speaking, most mergers fall into three categories.

Horizontal Merger

This occurs between two companies in the same industry. For example, two oil companies decide to merge because their belief is that they can create efficiencies within the company and, in turn, eliminate costs and improve profitability. This would inevitably cause valuation to increase, because profitability is a key driver of valuation. In doing this, the two companies have achieved some synergy, and this horizontal merger makes sense.

Vertical Merger

This occurs between two companies involved in different stages of production. Suppose two companies in the media production industry decide to merge. One produces content, and the other owns a network with vast distribution capabilities. This results in the perfect formula for a successful vertical merger, with content and delivery now offered from one company. Ultimately, the different stages of production delivery combine to create more efficiency, more productivity, more profitability, and, of course, more value.

Conglomerate Merger

This occurs between companies in often unrelated industries that seek to create a diversified portfolio of companies intended to hedge against risk. This type of merger can also create some operating efficiencies resulting from the combination of redundant departments.

Why Merge?

Mergers, ultimately, are driven by the quest for improved valuation. This goal manifests itself through the often used, and more often misunderstood, concept of synergy. Synergy, in its purest form, is based on a simple formula: Company A, when added to Company B, has to create a Company AB, whose value or productivity exceeds that of the two individual parts treated as separate entities. In other words, 1 plus 1 equals 3.

For example, suppose Company A is valued at $20 billion. Company B is valued at $15 billion. The managers of the two companies believe that if they merge to create Company AB, they will achieve the following:

- Reduced operating expenses
- Better purchasing power with suppliers
- Tax benefits
- Lower costs of financing

- Stronger brand awareness
- Cross-promotional opportunities

If all goes according to plan, these changes should lead to increased profits, stronger growth, and ultimately better value for shareholders. In fact, if the market believes that this will be achieved, the combined market value of the merged entity may be substantially more than the $35 billion if the two companies stayed separate. So when two companies combine, they seek to create synergy that justifies the need to merge.

The goal of any merger is to ultimately create additional value for shareholders. Some of the specific opportunities that might lead to this are detailed below.

Utilize Surplus Funds

Cash-rich firms might use cash to fund acquisitions in an effort to generate long-term growth. It is a means by which they can rid themselves of excess cash while creating additional growth opportunities. For example, an oil service company might acquire a technologically strong logistics company with significant upside potential. This oil service company is working with a good deal of surplus cash, and by acquiring this logistics company, it improves its operating efficiency.

At the same time, cash-rich firms themselves often become targets of takeovers from larger firms that are seeking to build steady, consistent cash flows. For example, a mining company might acquire a steady cash flow construction company to hedge against risky mining projects. The mining company is accustomed to significant ups and downs within the industry; so to maintain steady reserves of cash, it might decide to acquire a construction company whose business is more predictable from a cash standpoint.

Eliminate Management Inefficiencies

The need or the decision to merge might often stem from the goal of eliminating management inefficiencies. Acquisition often creates opportunities to eliminate certain management teams and replace them with new ones. In doing this, the expectation is that bringing on new management with fresh ideas will eliminate old inefficiencies. Quite often, the simple public relations impact of such a move is enough to create some additional value for publicly traded companies.

Increase Revenues

Increases in revenue can arise from a number of sources, including better distribution, a diversified product mix, access to new markets, and access to new sales channels. Ultimately, anything resulting in a boost to the top line can be justification enough for a merger.

Decrease Costs and Expenses

A decrease in costs and expenses is the goal of virtually any type of merger. The decreases result from the greater efficiencies that occur through the consolidation of certain services. In many cases, the efficiencies arise from the consolidation of back-office operations such as office management, accounting, public relations, and marketing. By combining entities, companies can very often eliminate inefficiencies and decrease overhead.

Create Production Efficiencies

Companies will very often seek some competitive advantage by optimizing the production process, and a merger is frequently the best way to achieve this. This can be facilitated through the efficient coordination of the administration or delivery of a certain business product or business unit. For example, a shipping company that leases ships may look to purchase or acquire a company that already owns these ships. This might eliminate some of those inefficiencies involved with the delivery of the leasing process.

Realize Tax Benefits

Of course, there are often tax benefits resulting from mergers. Tax gains provide powerful incentives, especially for multibillion dollar corporations. Firms with net tax losses can be attractive targets for an acquirer with a significant tax burden. These tax losses or even tax credits can be used to offset the tax burden of the acquirer. Also, a firm with unused debt capacity can be an attractive takeover target because of the tax savings that result from additional debt financing. Plus, sometimes there is an opportunity to write up certain depreciable assets. As shown earlier, tax deductions are often generated through additional depreciation.

Reduce Capital Expenditures

Mergers can also reduce combined capital expenditure. If Firm A needs new manufacturing facilities and Firm B has excess manufacturing capacity, a merger might eliminate Firm A's capital requirements to build or expand. Mergers can also create working capital efficiencies for both firms. The merger might create more liquidity, liquidity that could be deployed in near-term initiatives. So the merger might actually create certain opportunities to sell off select assets that are not required by the combined firm. That, in and of itself, could create additional value.

Lower Financing Costs

Mergers can lead to lower financing costs. By acquiring a company with a strong credit rating, the credit rating of the new entity would be better than that of the acquirer company. Therefore, this would help lower the overall cost of financing.

Valuation

The reasons to merge outlined above might make strategic sense, and all it takes is a smooth-talking CEO with a minor in drama to impress the masses. However, convincing Wall Street is another story. Enter the bean counters. By projecting cost savings and revenue enhancements resulting from a merger, a detailed financial model can make the case for a merger. For example, in determining whether or not there is a justifiable reason to merge, they would look at present values for the proposed merged entity. The first step would be to forecast cash flows for the merged entity. Then, if the present value of the merged entity's cash flow exceeds the current market values for the individual companies, they've got a good case to merge.

Another way to assess the viability of a merger from a financial standpoint is to take the projected additional cash flows that would result from the merger and discount them to present value. The sum of these discounted cash flows is then subtracted from the investment amount needed for the acquisition. This is a standard net present value calculation that was covered earlier in the book. If the net present value is greater than zero, the merger makes sense. If it is less than zero, well . . .

Now this can all be problematic if companies simply rely on this one type of analysis to justify their case. Many other assumptions are involved, some that are quantifiable and others that are not, such as management or management's ability to deliver the expected benefits.

Example. Suppose Firm A and Firm B are competitors. Both firms have after-tax cash flows of $100 per year and a cost of capital of 10%. Firm A decides to acquire Firm B, with the expectation that after-tax cash flows of the newly combined entity would be $210 per year. Does this merger make sense? In this example, analysts can see that the cash flows from the merged entity are $210 per year, while the combined cash flows of the separate firms equaled $200 a year. There is an incremental gain in cash flow of $10. The value of the merged firm, assuming that these cash flows stay constant and applying the perpetuity formula to value them, would be $2,100. If each part was valued separately, the combined value would be $2,000. So by merging the firms, an additional $100 in value is created. That value captures the synergy that was reflected in the incremental cash flow gain.

These are some of the types of analyses that would be used to determine if this merger makes sense. Indeed, this is a somewhat simplistic look at merger analysis, but it sets forth the basic principles needed to determine financial viability.

Defenses

Any discussion of mergers and acquisitions deserves some mention of the many defense tactics that companies use to avoid being acquired. First, consider why a company's management might consider such defensive options. For starters, they might seek to extract a higher price from the acquiring company. At the same time, they could preserve jobs that would otherwise be lost if the merger went through. Or perhaps they are simply concerned with preserving the foundation and purpose of the company.

Company managers often consider the following options in crafting their defense strategy.

Poison Pills

Poison pills work when existing shareholders are issued rights to purchase additional shares of stock in the company at a bargain price during a takeover attempt. This effectively creates a dilutive impact on the number of shares outstanding and makes it difficult for the acquiring company to take over the target company at a reasonable price.

Poison Puts

Poison puts occur when bondholders demand repayment if there is a change of control as a result of a hostile takeover. This effectively raises the overall price of the acquisition.

Golden Parachutes

Golden parachute payouts offer hefty compensation packages to corporate managers, which can dissuade a cost-conscious acquirer.

Supermajority

Supermajority provisions push a simple majority requirement for merger approval to upward of 80% of outstanding voting rights needed to approve a merger.

Pac-Man

The Pac-Man defense is modeled after the famous video game, whereby a target company turns and acquires its would-be buyer.

Pac-Man defense and Bendix. The best example of a Pac-Man defense in M&A history was the attempted hostile takeover of Martin Marietta by Bendix Corporation in 1982. At the time, Martin Marietta was a diversified corporate giant with holdings in aerospace, electronics, and cement, while Bendix was a leader in air navigation systems. In response to Bendix's hostile overtures, Martin Marietta started buying Bendix stock with the intention of assuming control over the company. Bendix simultaneously persuaded Allied Corporation to act as a white knight, and the company was sold to Allied the same year.

Donkey Kong

Not widely recognized, but one that I'm sure could happen if the target company simply clobbered its would-be buyer over the head.

Greenmail and Mesa

In 1982, Mesa Petroleum, owned by Texas wildcat T. Boone Pickens, started acquiring shares of Cities Petroleum. To dissuade Pickens, Cities issued more shares of stock to dilute the current pool, making it more difficult for him to acquire control. Mesa then upped its bid for shares of Cities. Meanwhile, Cities decided to take the offensive and responded by making a bid for Mesa. In the end, Mesa pulled its bid for Cities and agreed not to make another bid for at least five years. Cities agreed to purchase the shares that Mesa originally acquired— earning Mesa an $80 million profit. Mesa went on to bid for Gulf and Phillips, each time losing, but also earning sizable profits through buyback agreements. In total, T. Boone Pickens made nearly $1 billion through failed takeover attempts and earned a reputation as the world's best "greenmailer" (someone who profits from a more refined form of blackmail).

Merger Obstacles

Invariably, mergers face a number of obstacles, including compliance with regulatory bodies and the overriding difficulties of integrating distinct business cultures.

Legal Issues

One of the biggest impediments to an effective merger is the web of legal issues that can easily slow, if not halt, the entire merger process. Among other things, corporations must address the following when engaged in a merger:

Compliance with federal, state, or local statutes regarding antitrust issues. In the United States, the Clayton Act prohibits a corporation from acquiring assets of another company if it substantially "lessens competition or tends to create a monopoly." For example, acquiring suppliers or customers may close the market to competition or may create an interindustry behemoth that eliminates new entrants. Similar principles are observed in larger overseas markets, and in fact, the European Union has blocked a number of high-profile mergers for these reasons.

Compliance with the DOJ and FTC. Both the Department of Justice and the Federal Trade Commission can take an active role in determining if a proposed merger can lead to issues of anticompetitiveness. The review process can be exhaustive and ultimately costly to all parties involved.

SEC filings. All proper documentation must be filed with the SEC in order for publicly traded companies to complete a merger or acquisition.

Employee benefits. Because employee benefits are often altered in a merger or acquisition, the proper legal protocol must be observed to ensure that employees receive their granted benefits. Oversights in this area can lead to costly lawsuits.

Foreign ownership. Federal law restricts ownership of certain assets by non-U.S. entities. In particular, certain aircraft manufacturers, telecom facilities, newspapers, nuclear power plants, and defense businesses are regulated by this.

Integration Issues

Integrating the merger often creates insurmountable problems. Integration issues, in fact, have contributed to the failure of several large corporate mergers. It is not uncommon for a new merged entity to exhibit the following:

- Clashes among managers
- Loss of key employees
- Unforeseen costs
- Drop in employee morale
- Difficulty with systems integration

Mergers Gone Wild

Biggest merger = biggest failure?

". . . we do believe we're on the path of building what may be the most valuable company and most respected company in the world someday, and we're going to continue to focus on making that happen."
**—Steve Case, former CEO,
AOL–Time Warner, January 12, 2000**

The largest corporate merger in history is becoming widely regarded as the biggest corporate failure in history—funny how that works. In 2001, AOL merged with Time Warner in a deal worth approximately $350 billion. The new company, AOL-Time Warner, brought forth the convergence of media, entertainment, and the Internet. Through the merger, AOL would gain access to Time Warner's broadband content delivery, as well as content from magazines, movies, music, and television. Time Warner, after several failed Internet initiatives, would now have access to AOL's 28 million subscribers. The story culminated in the eventual write-down of nearly $100 billion in goodwill, a painful reminder of how corporate mergers are all too often overvalued.

What happened? Among other things, the enormous size and scope of AOL-Time Warner (90,000 employees) proved difficult to manage. Specifically, the size of the new company proved unwieldy in responding to the characteristically rapid changes occurring in the Internet market. Additionally, merging a high-tech company with a media conglomerate created cultural issues, while failure to achieve economies of scope (i.e., cross-promotional marketing) proved costly. A number of analytical oversights that caused further problems included poor assessment of Time Warner's broadband systems, which proved to be geographically limited, thus hampering AOL's expansion plans. Finally, both companies were overvalued during the tech bubble, and both suffered as a result of stock market correction.

Leveraged Buyouts

Leveraged buyouts, or LBOs, are essentially an extension of mergers and acquisitions, the difference being that LBOs are acquisitions that are heavily financed through large amounts of debt. They gained prominence in the 1980s when companies issued heavy amounts of debt to acquire assets of seemingly undervalued companies. The goal of such transactions was that through an LBO, the target company could achieve some cost benefit or some level of efficiency. This strategy evolved over time to the point where the goal of an LBO is to simply achieve the highest return on investment in the shortest period of time. Nowadays, large private equity firms, or LBO shops, acquire distressed assets through the issuance of heavy amounts of debt with the intention of either revitalizing these assets or, quite often, selling them off piece by piece for higher returns at some point in the future.

LBOs were traditionally financed with high-yield (junk) bonds, which were at the time an easy source of financing, albeit a costly one. Typically, LBOs are financed with more than 50% senior bank debt, with a lesser portion of public debt, and with an even lesser portion of equity. In most LBOs, management not only takes an active interest in the structuring of the deal, but is often involved in the ongoing management of the company.

The LBO Model

The LBO financial model involves some of the following inputs, among which is the purchase price of the overall asset. This is a key driver of the distribution between debt and equity. Unlike any other type of financial model, the actual split between debt and equity becomes increasingly important because it does dictate how much is returned to the investors.

The acquiring company also looks at the projected income statement and the balance sheet for the target company to see how the returns will impact the overall financial health of the company. Aside from the general returns, the overall financial impact on the balance sheet can impact the future sale price.

The LBO model seeks to address the following questions:

- How much is a reasonable price to offer for the business?
- What percentage of the deal makes sense for the buyer?
- How sensitive are returns to performance targets?
- How will negative performance impact bank deals?
- If the business plateaus, how will this affect the overall returns?

In the next example, assume a company has the opportunity to acquire a new store. This store costs $100 million. It is expected that this investment will generate cash flows of $8 million a year for the next five years. Further assume that this real estate value is expected to increase in value at a rate of 3% per year for each of the next five years. Finally, assume a discount rate of 10%. Based on these assumptions, what is the net present value (NPV) of this opportunity? Figure 11.1 depicts the calculation.

In calculating NPV, first observe the cash flows in Figure 11.1. The acquiring company has a negative cash flow of $100 million in the current year. This is the amount of its initial investment. In subsequent years, there is the $8 million in cash flow achieved in years one through five, plus the projected value

NPV Calculation*

Year	0	1	2	3	4	5
Cash flows ($)	−100	8	8	8	8	124 (8 plus value of real estate after 5 years)
Present value ($)	−100.0	7.3	6.6	6.0	5.5	76.9
NPV ($)	2					
Discount rate	10%					

*Cash flow and NPV in millions.

Figure 11.1   Calculation of Net Present Value in the LBO Financial Model

of the store in year five, which yields a total cash flow in year five of $124 million. A present value calculation can be run based on a discount rate of 10%. In doing this, the resulting year one cash flow in present value terms is $7.3 million; year two, $6.6 million; year three, $6.0 million; year four, $5.5 million; and year five, the $8 million in cash flow plus the sale price of that real estate, which works out to a present value of $76.9 million. When these present value cash flows are added and the difference between the initial investment and these cash flows is taken, the net present value is $2 million.

Once the third variable, leverage, is introduced, the model is complete. What happens now if the acquirer can borrow 80% of the purchase price at an interest rate of 5%? Figure 11.2 shows the numbers. After servicing that debt, the net cash flow is reduced to $4 million per year. However, the initial investment is now only $20 million. So in doing this, the net present value increases to $17 million. This reflects the power of leverage, which is a key driver in such transactions.

- **Our net cash flows reduce to $4 million, but our initial investment is only $20 million.**
- **The opportunity reveals the power of leverage.**

NPV Calculation*

Year	0	1	2	3	4	5
Cash flows ($)	−20	4	4	4	4	40 (4 plus value of real estate after 5 years less debt outstanding)
Present value ($)	−20.0	3.6	3.3	3.0	2.7	24.8
NPV ($)	17					
Discount rate	10%					
Of the $100 million purchase price, the company borrowed $80 million. Cost of borrowing 5%. Now, a $20 million investment becomes more compelling.						

*Cash flow and NPV in millions.

Figure 11.2 Calculation of Net Present Value, Showing Leverage Variable, in the LBO Financial Model

RJR Nabisco LBO

Perhaps the most famous leveraged buyout in history was the takeover of RJR Nabisco. In 1988, the RJR board revealed that F. Ross Johnson, the company's CEO, had formed an investor group seeking to acquire company stock for $75 per share. Johnson's group was backed by Shearson Lehman, which at the time was a subsidiary of American Express. Upon this announcement, RJR's stock price moved from $56 to $75, giving shareholders a 36% gain over its last stock price. Once the company was in play, a number of other investors arrived. In fact, that initial bid of $75 was trumped by KKR's offer of $90, which included $79 in cash plus $11 in preferred stock. One month later, bidding closed. At this time, KKR had raised its bid to $109—$81 of which was based on cash, another $10 of which was based on convertible subordinate debentures, and $18 of which was preferred stock. Johnson's group offered more, $112 in cash and securities. Yet the RJR board eventually chose KKR. Why? The board believed that Johnson's valuations were softer and used loose assumptions. Furthermore, KKR's asset sales were less severe. What KKR had projected, as is the case in many leveraged buyouts, was the sale of certain assets to boost cash flows and pay down debt. Furthermore, KKR's operational plan tended to be more efficient. Finally, the board believed that Johnson's management compensation was overly generous.

So how could this move from $56 per share, just prior to the first announcement, to $109 per share be justified? KKR and other investors were betting on the benefits from certain interest tax shields, lower capital expenditure, and the sale of certain assets. In fact, the asset sales were expected to generate some $5 billion alone, and some of this included the sale of the corporate jets, affectionately termed the "RJR Air Force."

Conclusion

So there you have it—the good, the bad, and the ugly of finance and accounting. Although you may not be quite ready to structure the Coke-Pepsi merger or audit GE's financial statements, you have, hopefully, acquired a better understanding of what the so-called experts do. No longer will you wallow in ignorance when your favorite stock is downgraded, your company is acquired, or your boss is hauled off to jail for accounting fraud. And although you have gobbled up a number of complex concepts in a short period of time, don't be afraid to review them periodically or refer to them when needed. My goal was not to turn you into a financial wizard but rather to give you an insider's perspective of the world of accounting and finance. If you have come away with an appreciation for these concepts, great. And if you are skeptical, even better. It pays to question these concepts, and more importantly, the people who perpetuate them. Take nothing for granted, and be prepared to challenge them. Because we failed to do this before, we learned some important, albeit costly, lessons.

Case Study
Car-E-Oki, Inc.

Chapter 10 introduced you to Car-E-Oki, that up-and-coming company that is hoping to bring karaoke to automobiles and other vehicles. This appendix presents the typical documents you should study if you were thinking about investing in Car-E-Oki—or any other company.

Shred & Burn, CPAs

Cayman Islands

The Board of Directors and Shareholders
Car-E-Oki, Inc.:

We have audited the accompanying consolidated balance sheets of Car-E-Oki, Inc., and subsidiaries as of December 31, 2005, and December 31, 2004, and the related consolidated statements of operations, shareholders' equity, and cash flows for each of the years in the two-year period ended December 31, 2005. These consolidated financial statements are the responsibility of the Company's management. Our responsibility is to express an opinion on these consolidated financial statements based on our audits.

We conducted our audits in accordance with the standards of the Public Company Accounting Oversight Board (United States). Those standards require that we plan and perform the audit to obtain reasonable assurance about whether the financial statements are free of material misstatement. An audit includes examining, on a test basis, evidence supporting the amounts and disclosures in the consolidated financial statements. An audit also includes assessing the accounting principles used and significant estimates made by management, as well as evaluating the overall financial statement presentation. We believe that our audits provide a reasonable basis for our opinion.

In our opinion, the consolidated financial statements referred to above present fairly, in all material respects, the financial position of Car-E-Oki, Inc., and subsidiaries as of December 31, 2005, and December 31, 2004, and the results of their operations and their cash flows for each of the years in the two-year period ended December 31, 2005, in conformity with U.S. generally accepted accounting principles.

Shred & Burn, CPAs

May 31, 2006

A sample auditor's report, not unlike those prepared for most publicly traded companies.

CONSOLIDATED BALANCE SHEETS

All numbers in thousands except per-share amounts

Three fiscal years ended December 31, 2005	2005	2004
ASSETS		
Current Assets:		
Cash	$887,851	$316,391
Accounts Receivable	38,048	13,736
Inventories	127,328	136,828
Prepaid Expenses & Other Assets	52,836	40,257
Total Current Assets	$1,106,063	$507,212
Fixed Assets:		
Motor Vehicles	115,601	101,605
Machinery & Equipment	23,143	21,343
Leasehold Improvements	19,619	19,619
Furniture & Fixtures	11,194	11,194
Total Fixed Assets	169,557	153,761
Accumulated Depreciation	(71,896)	(62,378)
Net Fixed Assets	97,661	91,383
Total Assets	$1,203,724	$598,595
LIABILITIES AND SHAREHOLDERS' EQUITY		
Current Liabilities:		
Bank Line of Credit	$59,050	$59,050
Notes Payable Bank	17,584	0
Notes Payable Other	11,782	15,410
Accounts Payable	105,035	89,107
Accrued Expenses and Other Liabilities	36,213	29,369
Total Current Liabilities	$229,664	$192,936
Notes Payable, Bank	27,232	10,000
Notes Payable, Other	24,546	27,516
Total Long-Term Debt	51,778	37,516
Total Liabilities	$281,442	$230,452
Stockholders' Equity:		
Paid-in Capital	11,000	11,000
Retained Earnings	911,282	357,143
Total Stockholder Equity	922,282	368,143
Total Liabilities and Equity	$1,203,724	$598,595

A standard format balance sheet depicting two years of performance, which is useful in determining trends.

CONSOLIDATED INCOME STATEMENT

All numbers in thousands except per-share amounts

Three fiscal years ended December 31, 2005	2005	2004
Net Sales	$2,171,451	$1,675,456
Cost of Goods Sold	654,325	543,604
Gross Profit	1,517,126	1,131,852
Selling, General, & Administrative Expenses	88,664	99,852
Total Operating Expenses	88,664	99,852
EBITDA	1,428,462	1,032,000
Depreciation	9,518	2,667
Earnings before Interest & Taxes	1,418,944	1,029,333
Interest Expense	14,758	10,654
Profit before Taxes	1,404,186	1,018,679
Income Taxes	505,507	366,724
Net Income	$898,679	$651,955
Average Shares Outstanding	2,000,000	2,000,000
Net Income/Share	$0.45	$0.33
NET INCOME	$898,679	$651,955
PLUS Beginning Retained Earnings	357,143	76,438
Distribution to Stockholders	(344,540)	(371,250)
Ending Retained Earnings	$911,282	$357,143

A standard income statement followed by a statement of retained earnings (last four lines), which captures the link between the balance sheet and income statement.

CONSOLIDATED STATEMENTS OF CASH FLOWS

All numbers in thousands except per-share amounts

Three fiscal years ended December 31, 2005	2005	2004
Cash Beginning of Period	316,391	9,781
Cash Flows from Operations:		
Net Income	$898,679	$651,955
Adjustments to Reconcile to Cash		
Provided (Used) in Operations		
Depreciation	9,518	2,667
Accounts Receivable	(24,312)	81,741
Inventory	9,500	(7,595)
Prepaid Expenses	(12,579)	(4,296)
Accounts Payable	15,928	8,202
Accrued Expenses and Other Liabilities	6,844	(12,056)
Net Cash Flow from Operations	903,578	720,618
Cash Flows from Investing:		
Purchase of Fixed Assets	(15,796)	(14,920)
Cash Flows from Financing:		
Borrowings (Repayment) of Bank Credit Line	$0	($14,200)
Borrowings (Repayment) of Notes Payable, Bank	34,816	0
Borrowings (Repayment) of Notes Payable, Other	(6,598)	(13,638)
Distribution to Stockholders	(344,540)	(371,250)
Cash Flows from Financing	(316,322)	(399,088)
NET Increase (Decrease) in Cash	571,460	306,610
Cash End of Period	**$887,851**	**$316,391**

A standard cash flow statement, which is used to document changes in cash position. The ending cash balance forms the link between the cash flow statement and the balance sheet.

Press Release   Source: Car-E-Oki, Inc.

Car-E-Oki Reports Third Quarter Results
February 23, 2006 4:30 pm ET

Car-E-Oki Delivers Record Revenue & Earnings

CUPERTINO, Calif., February 23 /PRNewswire-FirstCall/ Car-E-Oki® today announced financial results for its fiscal year ended December 31, 2005, reporting the highest revenue and earnings in the Company's history. Car-E-Oki posted a net profit of $898 million, or $.45 per diluted share, and revenue of $2.17 billion. These results compare to a net profit of $651 million, or $.33 per diluted share, and revenue of $1.67 billion in the prior year, and represent revenue growth of 29 percent and net profit growth of 38 percent. Gross margin was 70 percent, up from 68 percent in the prior year. International sales accounted for 39 percent of the revenue.

Car-E-Oki shipped 11,182,000 iCroons units during the year, representing 35 percent growth over the prior year.

"We are delighted to report Car-E-Oki's best quarter ever in both revenue and earnings," said Cancion Fuerte, Car-E-Oki's CEO. "The launch of these new products has been a tremendous success, and we have more amazing new products in the pipeline. We're very pleased to report 29 percent revenue growth and a 38 percent increase in net income."

Car-E-Oki will provide live streaming of its 2005 financial results conference call. The live webcast will begin at 2:00 p.m. PDT on February 24, 2006, at http://www.Car-E-Oki.com.

This press release contains forward-looking statements about future products and the Company's estimated revenue and earnings for the fourth quarter of fiscal 2005. These statements involve risks and uncertainties, and actual results may differ. Potential risks and uncertainties include continued competitive pressures in the marketplace; the effect competitive and economic factors and the Company's reaction to them may have on consumer and business buying decisions with respect to the Company's products; the ability of the Company to make timely delivery of new products and successful technological innovations to the marketplace; the continued availability on acceptable terms of certain components and services essential to the Company's business currently obtained by the Company from sole or limited sources; the effect that the Company's dependency on manufacturing and logistics services provided by third parties may have on the quality, quantity, or cost of products manufactured or services rendered; the Company's reliance on the availability of third-party music content. More information on potential factors that could affect the Company's financial results is included from time to time in the Company's public reports filed with the SEC, including the Company's Form 10-K or the Company's Form 10-Q. The Company assumes no obligation to update any forward-looking statements or information, which speak as of their respective dates.

A quarterly earnings press release highlighting earnings per share and key growth drivers.

BULL - STEARNS

T. Jones
(555) 555-8546
tjones@bull.com

B. Smith
(555) 555-9208
bsmith@bull.com

Equity Research
IT Hardware / Rated: Strong Buy
July 29, 2006

Car-E-Oki, Inc. (CEO-20.00) - Strong Buy   Another Big Upside for Mobile Music; Well Positioned for Future Growth

Data

| Target Price-Yr.End '06 | $31 | Current Market Cap (000s) | $40,000,000 | Shares Out (000s) | **2,000,000** |

Pro Forma Estimates

	Q1 Dec	Q2 Mar	Q3 Jun	Q4 Sep	Year	P/E Year
2006	$0.15	$0.23	$0.39	$0.52	$1.29	24
2007	$0.17	$0.25	$0.43	$0.57	$1.42	22
2008	$0.18	$0.28	$0.47	$0.63	$1.56	20

Decision Points

- This stock is a must own. Car-E-Oki in-dash system experiencing strong double-digit sales growth.
- New product launches include: Boat-E-Oki, Bike-E-Oki, Board-E-Oki (for skaters and surfers).
- Halo effect from flagship car brand will enhance sales of other products.
- Advent of Car-E-Oki casting will allow for on-road duets further fueling the phenomenon.
- Discussions in place with major airlines for Plane-E-Oki although pilots' unions demand right of first refusal on song collection.

Industry Outlook

Growth prospects abound with few new entrants in the market. Car-E-Oki's plan to expand to other verticals (i.e., boating, biking, boarding) should solidify its presence as a preeminent player in the global karaoke market. As one senior manager stated, "People around the world will be belting out their favorite tunes on Car-E-Oki machines, and in a few years, people will be singing in unison wherever you go."

Revenue Growth

We expect Car-E-Oki to continue to exhibit double-digit top-line growth due to the following markets initiatives:
- Expansion into new products (boating, biking, boarding).
- Expansion overseas—namely, the Asian markets were the earliest adopters of traditional karaoke machines. Rollouts to Japan, Korea, and China planned within the next two years.
- Expansion to new demographics targeting the lucrative under-four market with Toddler-Oki.

Reiterate Buy with Price Target

CEO is undervalued at current levels. We reiterate our strong buy rating with a price target of $31.

A sample Wall Street equity research report highlighting earnings forecasts, industry outlook, revenue drivers, and price target (based on valuation).

Comparable Multiple Valuation

Prices on a per-share basis
All numbers in thousands except per-share amounts

	Share Price	Earnings/Share	P/E
Musica Buena S.A.	$72	$2.00	36
Mr. Roboto Corp.	$48	$3.00	16
Vegas Sounds, Inc.	$64	$4.00	16
Canadian Idol Studios	$54	$2.00	27
Industry average			24
C.E.O.	?	$1.29	

Industry P/E × company earnings = company fair value

24 × $1.29 = $31

$31 × 2,000,000 shares = $62,000,000

A sample valuation model used to determine the price target on an equity research report.

INCOME STATEMENT PROJECTIONS

All numbers in thousands, except per-share amounts

Three fiscal years ended December 31, 2008	2006	2007	2008
Net Sales	$9,258,118	$10,183,930	$11,202,323
Cost of Goods Sold	4,681,408	5,150,163	5,710,176
Gross Profit	$4,576,710	$ 5,033,767	$ 5,492,147
Selling, General, & Administrative Expenses	518,450	$ 587,834	$ 601,238
Operating Income	4,058,260	4,445,933	4,890,909
Depreciation	10,500	10,500	10,500
Earnings before Interest & Taxes	$4,047,760	$ 4,435,433	$ 4,880,409
Interest Expense	9,980	9,980	9,980
Profit before Taxes	$4,037,780	$ 4,425,453	$ 4,870,429
Income Taxes	1,453,601	1,593,163	1,753,354
Net Income	$2,584,179	$ 2,832,290	$ 3,117,075
Average Shares Outstanding	2,000,000	2,000,000	2,000,000
Net Income/Share	$1.29	$1.42	$1.56
NET INCOME	$2,584,179	$2,832,290	$3,117,075
PLUS Beginning Retained Earnings	911,282	3,150,921	5,638,671
Distribution to Stockholders	(344,540)	(344,540)	(344,540)
Ending Retained Earnings	$3,150,921	$5,638,671	$8,411,206

Sample income statement projections used to derive pro forma earnings.

Analyzing Car-E-Oki, Inc.

Activity Ratios

	2005	2004
Inventory turnover days = 365/(cost of goods sold/average inventory)	74 days	89 days
Accounts receivable turnover days = 365/(credit sales/average accounts receivables)	9 days	24 days
Accounts payable turnover days = 365/(purchases/average accounts payable)	55 days	56 days

Cost of goods sold	$654,325	$543,604
Average inventory (average of last year and this year)	$132,078	$133,031
Credit sales (assume 50% of total sales)	$1,085,726	$837,728
Average accounts receivables (average of last year and this year)	$25,892	$54,607
Purchases (cost of goods sold + change in inventory)	$644,825	$551,199
Average accounts payables (average of last year and this year)	$97,071	$85,006

Overall, the activity ratios of CEO reveal that the company is showing slight improvement in its ability to turn inventory, with dramatic improvement in its ability to collect receivables. These improvements, combined with a stable turnover of payables, are helping the company achieve the highest levels of activity efficiency.

Liquidity Ratios

	2005	2004
Current ratio = current assets/current liabilities	4.82	2.63
Quick ratio = (cash + marketable securities + accounts receivable)/current liabilities	4.03	1.71
Cash ratio = (cash + marketable securities)/current liabilities	3.87	1.64

The company continues to show improving liquidity ratios and is well above the industry averages. The cash ratio alone reveals sufficient cash reserves to cover any near-term liabilities.

Long-Term Debt and Solvency Ratios

	2005	2004
Debt-to-capital ratio = total debt/(total debt + total equity)	13%	23%
Debt-to-equity = total debt/total equity	15%	30%
Times interest earned = EBIT/interest	96.15	96.61
Additional Information:		
Total debt (lines of credit + short- and long-term debt)	$140,194	$111,976
Total equity (shareholders' equity)	$922,282	$368,143

The company shows declining debt levels and a strong ability to service what little debt exists. We believe, however, that the company should consider issuing more debt to bring it in line with industry standards. Proceeds from a debt issuance could be used for expansion efforts as well as share buybacks.

Profit Ratios

	2005	2004
Gross margin = gross profit/sales	69.9%	67.6%
Operating margin = operating income/sales	65.8%	61.6%
Profit margin = net income/sales	41.4%	38.9%

The company continues to show steadily improving profit margins that are among the highest in the industry. Concerns over new entrants have raised speculation that strong gross margins will not continue indefinitely. The company has issued statements regarding this but promised to initiate any required operating expense reductions to keep operating margins strong.

Return Analysis

	2005	2004
Return on assets = net income/total assets	75%	109%
Return on total capital = net income/(total debt + total equity)	85%	136%
Return on equity = net income/total equity	97%	177%
Additional Information:		
Total debt (lines of credit + short- and long-term debt)	$140,194	$111,976
Total equity (shareholders' equity)	$922,282	$368,143

Returns on assets, capital, and book equity are strong although declining gradually. Although the company appears healthy overall, this underperformance raises questions about the company's sustainable growth prospects.

Market Analysis

	2005	2004
Price-to-earnings ratio = stock price/earnings per share	45	31
Earnings yield = earnings per share/market price per share	2%	3%
Dividend yield = dividends per share/market price per share	0.86%	1.86%
Dividend payout ratio = dividends per share/earnings per share	38%	57%
Price-to-book ratio = market price/book price	43	54
Additional Information:		
Stock price (price per share at year end)	$20.00	$10.00
Earnings per share	$0.45	$0.33
Dividend per share (dividend/shares outstanding)	0.17	0.19
Market price (stock price per share)	$20.00	$10.00
Book price (shareholders' equity/shares outstanding)	$0.46	$0.18

CEO has seen a near doubling of its stock price each year for the last four years. However, double-digit increases in earnings reflect the fact that growth is consistently priced into the stock, and yet the company has been slow to achieve fair value. Nonetheless, we believe that this will be the year for CEO, and as such, we are reiterating our recommendation of STRONG BUY and holding our year-end price target of $31 a share. With new products and new markets on the horizon, it won't be long before the Car-E-Oki machine is as common as the seatbelt in most cars. And this does not include the potential for other vehicles. Combine this with a strong balance sheet, solid cash flows, and increasing profits, and we have a formula for success.

Sample Problems

Financial Statements Problem

This problem set is an effective way to capture the relationship between the balance sheet, income statement, and cash flow statement. First, construct an income statement to arrive at net income. This will form the starting point for the cash flow statement, which takes into account the changes in cash.

Problem: Help your client with his finances by organizing the following into an income statement and cash flow statement. Make sure to include:

Sales
Expenses
Cash Flow from Operations
Cash Flow from Investing
Cash Flow from Financing
Net Change in Cash

T. Soprano Associates (*Note:* Not Intended for IRS use)	
Entertainment Division Revenues	$ 70,000
Construction Revenues	$100,000
Sports Revenues	$ 80,000
Increased Accounts Receivable	$ 70,000
Increased Merchandise Inventory	$ 20,000
Depreciation	$ 20,000
Increased Accounts Payable	
Liquor Suppliers	$ 40,000
Cement Suppliers	$ 4,000
Increased Salaries Payable	$ 2,000
Cost of Goods Sold	$120,000
Salaries	$ 40,000
Interest	$ 8,000
Other expenses	$ 22,000
Taxes	NA
Acquisition of Buildings and Equipment	$250,000
Dividends Paid	$ 16,000
Proceeds from Long-Term Debt Issued	$100,000
"Loans from Friends"	
Net Change in Cash for Year	?
Cash, January 1	$160,000
Cash, December 31	?

Financial Statements Solution

Income Statement

Sales		
Entertainment Division		$ 70,000
Construction		$100,000
Sports		$ 80,000
	Total Sales	$250,000
Less Expenses		
Cost of Goods Sold		$120,000
Salaries		$ 40,000
Depreciation		$ 20,000
Interest		$ 8,000
Other Expenses		$ 22,000
	Total Costs and Expenses	$210,000
Net Income		$ 40,000

Cash Flow Statement

Operations	
Net Income	$ 40,000
Additions	
Depreciation	$ 20,000
Increased Accounts Payable	
Liquor Suppliers	$ 40,000
Cement Suppliers	$ 4,000
Increased Salaries Payable	$ 2,000
Subtractions	
Increased Accounts Receivable	$ (70,000)
Increased Merchandise Inventory	$ (20,000)
Cash Flow from Operations	$ 16,000
Investing	
Acquisition of Buildings and Equipment	$(250,000)
Financing	
Dividends Paid	$ (16,000)
Proceeds from Long-Term Debt Issued "Loans from Friends"	$100,000
Cash Flow from Financing	$ 84,000
Net Change in Cash for Year	$(150,000)
Cash, January 1	$ 160,000
Cash, December 31	$ 10,000

Valuation Problem

Compare valuation numbers based on the discounted cash flow method and comparable multiple method—this is standard practice in most M&A transactions.

Part A   AB Pharmaceuticals has invented a new drug to eliminate those unsightly wrinkles that form around the elbow with age. The new drug, Elbowtox, is expected to revolutionize the market for elbow rejuvenation products. It's rival company, Pharmacia ZY, has launched a hostile bid for AB and asked that you construct a discounted cash flow analysis to help evaluate this acquisition. The cash flows created as a result of this transaction are detailed below:

	Year 1	Year 2	Year 3	Year 4	Year 5
Incremental cash flows	$500,000	$800,000	$1,100,000	$1,300,000	$1,500,000
Discount rate (r)	10%				

Note: Year 5 and beyond, cash flows remain flat.

a. What is the value of the gain from this merger?_____
b. If the acquisition price is $5 million, what is the NPV?____

Part B   Looking at the acquisition on a comparable basis, what would be a fair price for AB?

	Share Price	Earnings/Share	P/E
ZY	24	$2.00	12
CD	36	$1.00	36
EF	66	$3.00	22
GH	30	$1.50	20
Industry average			22.5
AB	?	$2.00	

a. The share price for AB should be: _____
b. With 100,000 shares outstanding, a fair price
   would be: _____

Valuation Solution

Part A

	Year 1	Year 2	Year 3	Year 4	Year 5
Incremental cash flows	$500,000	$800,000	$1,100,000	$1,300,000	$1,500,000
PV	$454,545	$661,157	$826,446	$887,917	$931,382
Discount rate (r)	10%				
Terminal value year 5	$15,000,000				
Terminal value today	$9,313,820				

Note: Year 5 and beyond, cash flows remain flat.

a. What is the value of the gain from this merger? $13,075,268

b. If the acquisition price is $5 million, what is the NPV? $8,075,268

Part B

	Share Price	Earnings/Share	P/E
ZY	24	$2.00	12
CD	36	$1.00	36
EF	66	$3.00	22
GH	30	$1.50	20
Industry average			22.5
AB	?	$2.00	

a. The share price for AB should be: $45.00

b. With 100,000 shares outstanding, a fair price would be: $4,500,000

Summary Formulas

Here is a handy guide to the main formulas found in the book.

Activity Analysis

Use these to evaluate revenues and output generated by the firm's assets:

Inventory turnover days = 365/(cost of goods sold/average inventory)

Accounts receivable turnover days = 365/(credit sales/average accounts receivables)

Accounts payable turnover days = 365/(purchases/average accounts payable)

Liquidity Analysis

Use these to measure the adequacy of the firm's cash resources to meet its near-term cash obligations:

Current ratio = current assets/current liabilities
Quick ratio = (cash + marketable securities + accounts receivable)/current liabilities
Cash ratio = (cash + marketable securities)/current liabilities

Long-Term Debt and Solvency

These formulas are used to examine the firm's capital structure, including the mix of its financing sources and the ability of the firm to satisfy its longer-term debt and investment obligations:

Debt-to-capital ratio = total debt/(total debt + total equity)
Debt to equity = total debt/total equity
Times interest earned = earnings before interest & taxes/interest

Profitability Analysis

Use these when you want to measure the relationship between a firm's costs and its sales:

Gross margin = gross credit/sales
Operating margin = operating income/sales
Profit margin = net income/sales

Return Analysis

These measure the relationship between profits and the investment required to generate them:

Return on assets = net income/total assets
Return on total capital = net income/ (total debt + total equity)
Return on equity = net income/total equity

Market Analysis

Here are formulas you can use to measure value, income, and dividends relative to one another:

Price-to-earnings ratio = stock price/earnings per share
Earnings yield = earnings per share/market price per share
Dividend yield = dividends per share/market price per share
Dividend payout ratio = dividends per share/earnings per share
Price-to-book ratio = market price/book price

Time Value of Money

This allows you to calculate present value for a single amount. The formula is for present value (PV) of a lump sum (FV_n) given at the end of n period at an interest rate of r%, discounted once per period:

$$PV = FV_n/(1 + r)^n$$

Valuation

Valuation of an Asset

For this formula, we assume the value of an asset with expected cash flows CF_t at times $t = 1, 2, \ldots, n$, with required rate of return r:

$$\text{Value of asset} = \sum_{t=1}^{n} \text{cash} = \frac{CF_1}{(1+r)} + \frac{CF_2}{(1+r)^2} + \cdots + \frac{CF_n}{(1+r)^n}$$

Cost of Capital

Dividend Growth Model

$$r_E = (D_1/P_0) + g$$

where $D_1 = D_0 \times (1 + g)$
D_0 = most recent dividend payment
P_0 = current stock price
g = estimated dividend growth (use historical rates or analysts' forecasts)

Cost of Equity (r_E)

Using the capital asset pricing model (CAPM):

$$r_E = r_f = \beta \, (r_m - r_f)$$

where β = beta coefficient of the stock
r_f = risk-free rate
r_m = expected rate on the market portfolio

Weighted-Average Cost of Capital (WACC)

$$r_{\text{WACC}} = (1 - T)r_D D/V + r_E E/V$$

where T = tax rate
r_D = rate of return on debt
D = total debt outstanding in dollars
E = market value of equity in dollars
V = total value of company = $D + E$
r_E = rate of return on equity*

*Can derive using either the dividend discount model or CAPM.

Glossary

10-K A financial statement covering a company's annual performance to be filed with the Securities and Exchange Commission.

10-Q An unaudited statement of a company's quarterly performance that includes reports similar to those found in a 10-K.

accounts payable The amounts owed by a company to vendors or suppliers.

accounts receivable Payments owed to a company by customers.

accrual accounting The recording of transactions as they occur, rather than when the cash actually changes hands.

amortization The dispersion of expenses or payment for an obligation over an extended period of time.

annual report A condensed version of the 10-K, with more emphasis placed on marketing a company to investors through colorful charts and pictures.

arbitrage   The simultaneous purchase and sale of an asset or security to capitalize on price differentials that might exist between different marketplaces or exchanges.

assets   The resources of a company that are expected to yield some future benefit.

auditor's report   Report issued by an independent accounting firm hired to determine that the company's financial reports are in conformity with GAAP standards. Auditors are now required to disclose any red flags in their report.

book accounting   A system of financial reporting designed to comply with GAAP standards, but not necessarily with IRS rules and regulations.

call option   A contract that allows the holder to purchase a security at a fixed price within a specified period of time.

cash   The most liquid of all assets.

cash accounting   The recording of transactions when cash changes hands.

cash ratio   The ratio of cash and marketable securities to current liabilities; the current ratio with the exclusion of inventory and accounts receivable.

conglomerate merger   A merger that occurs between two companies in unrelated industries.

cost   What is paid to produce or acquire goods and services.

current assets   Liquid assets, those that can be most readily converted to cash, consumed, or sold (usually within one year).

current debt   Any type of short-term bond or note issued by a company.

current liabilities   Forms of short-term obligations, including lines of credit outstanding, accounts payable, current debt, and current portion of long-term debt.

current portion of long-term debt   The amount due in the present year on long-term issued debt.

current ratio   The most common measure of a company's liquidity, the ratio of current assets to current liabilities.

debt-to-capital ratio   The most common form of long-term debt and solvency analysis. The proportion of total debt relative to total debt and equity.

debt-to-equity ratio   The ratio of total debt to total equity.

depreciation   The loss of value of a fixed asset over its expected life.

derivative   A security based on the movement of some other underlying security or index.

direct owners' equity   The funds invested directly into the company by its shareholders; usually listed as *paid-in capital*.

dividend   A periodical payment made to shareholders in a company.

dividend payout ratio   The ratio of dividend per share to earnings per share.

dividend yield   The ratio of dividend per share to market price per share.

double entry accounting   An accounting system whereby every transaction occurring on one side of a financial statement has one or more accompanying transactions occurring elsewhere in the financial statements.

earnings release   A condensed form of the company's income statement that highlights the company's performance based on profits.

earnings yield   The ratio of earnings per share to market price per share of a company.

EBIT   Earnings before interest and taxes.

EBITDA   Earnings before interest, taxes, depreciation, and amortization.

EBT   Earnings before taxes.

economic value added (EVA)   A performance measure of a company that deducts cost of capital from tax-adjusted operating profit.

expenses   What is paid to run the company on a day-to-day basis.

FASB   Financial Accounting Standards Board. The overseeing body in charge of establishing and improving financial accounting and reporting standards.

FIFO   The first-in, first-out method of accounting for inventory in which the first good produced or purchased is the first one sold.

Form 144   A registration that discloses when insiders buy or sell stock.

Form 8-K   A form due to the SEC after any material event (any major change in ownership, capital structure, or auditor).

forward   A contractual obligation to transfer an asset at a specific price on a specific date.

future   A contract to buy or sell an underlying asset on a particular date.

GAAP   Generally Accepted Accounting Principles. The overall principles used in financial reporting.

goodwill   The difference between the price paid for an asset and its fair market value.

gross margin   The ratio of gross profit to sales.

horizontal merger   A merger that occurs between two companies in the same industry.

indirect owners' equity   Equity built up through the generation of income. Also known as *retained earnings.*

interest   A payment made to finance debt.

inventory   Goods that a company has produced or purchased but has yet to sell.

leveraged buyout (LBO)   An acquisitions that is financed through a large amount of debt.

liabilities   Obligations due in the future based on activities from the past; what the company owes.

LIFO   The last-in, first-out method of accounting for inventory in which the last good produced or purchased is the first one sold.

line of credit   The amount a company has drawn from any credit facilities, similar to credit cards in personal finance.

management's discussion and analysis (MD&A)   A strategic overview of a company's performance during the prior year, including expected changes for the coming year. Found at the beginning of most annual reports and 10-Ks for publicly traded companies.

management's report A supplement to the MD&A that details the responsibilities of the individual managers in preparing the financial reports.

marketable securities Short-term investments listed under current assets on the balance sheet.

money laundering The practice of taking money from illegal sources and passing it through a business to make the money appear legitimate.

net income A company's profit; the residual amount when all expenses and costs are subtracted from revenues.

net present value (NPV) The present value of future returns less the initial investment.

noncurrent assets Assets that cannot be liquidated within the course of one year.

noncurrent liabilities Any long-term debt that comes due after the course of one year.

operating income Revenue less expenses involved in the day-to-day operations of a business.

operating margin The ratio of operating income to sales.

option A contract that gives the owner the right to buy or sell something at a specified price within a specified period of time.

owners' equity The book value of a company; the difference between its assets and liabilities. Also known as *shareholders' equity*.

prepaid expense An expenditure for a good or service paid in advance of its due date; listed on the balance sheet and reduced as payments come due.

price-to-book ratio The ratio of market price per share to book price per share.

price-to-earnings ratio The ratio of stock price to earnings per share.

pro forma financials Any type of adjusted financial statement.

profit margin The ratio of net income to sales.

property, plant, and equipment (PP&E) See *tangible fixed assets*.

proxy statement A financial report, offered at a company's annual meeting, detailing management compensation, management stock options, related-party transactions, and auditor changes.

put option A contract that gives the holder the right to sell a security at a fixed price.

quick ratio The current ratio with inventory excluded from current assets.

retained earnings See *indirect owners' equity*.

return on assets The ratio of net income to total assets.

return on equity The ratio of net income to total equity.

return on total capital The ratio of net income to the sum of total debt and equity.

revenue Payments received in exchange for goods or services.

Securities and Exchange Commission (SEC) The independent regulatory agency of the U.S. government in charge of regulating all publicly traded companies.

selling, general, and administrative (SG&A) The day-to-day operating expenses of a company as listed on the income statement.

shareholders' equity See *owners' equity.*

swap A type of derivative in which two parties enter into an agreement to exchange their streams of cash flows.

tangible fixed assets Noncurrent assets, including all property, real estate, and equipment. Also know as *property, plant, and equipment (PP&E).*

tax accounting A system of financial reporting designed to ensure that income and deductions reported on tax returns are in compliance with IRS rules and regulations.

times interest earned ratio The ratio of EBIT to interest.

vertical merger A merger that occurs between two companies involved in different stages of production within an industry.

warrant A volatile option with a longer duration than a standard option that usually originates as part of a new bond issue.

Recommended Readings

Borghese, Robert J., and Paul Borghese, *M&A from Planning to Integration: Executing Acquisitions and Increasing Shareholder Value*, McGraw-Hill, New York, 2002.

Brealey, Richard A., and Stewart C. Myers, *Principles of Corporate Finance*, 6th ed., McGraw-Hill, New York, 2000.

Copeland, Tom, Tim Koller, and Jack Murrin, *Valuation: Measuring and Managing the Value of Companies*, Wiley, New York, 2000.

Ramesh, Ram, *Financial Analyst's Indispensable Pocket Guide*, McGraw-Hill, New York, 2001.

Rickertsen, Rick, *Buyout: The Insider's Guide to Buying Your Own Company*, New York, AMACOM, 2001.

Schilit, Howard, *Financial Shenanigans*, 2nd ed., McGraw-Hill, New York, 2002.

Index

About the Author

Reuben Advani is the founder and president of TeleStrat Consulting, Inc., a financial advisory boutique that specializes in corporate valuation. In addition, Mr. Advani launched a popular series of MBA-style seminars that are offered at corporations and law firms in the United States and Europe. Mr. Advani began his career with Morgan Stanley & Co., Inc., the Wall Street bank, where he worked in the firm's corporate finance division. In this capacity, he performed detailed valuation analysis on acquisition targets for Fortune 500 companies and oversaw the coordination of several debt and equity issuances. Mr. Advani's next position was with Sony Corporation of America, where he was active in the development of Sony's online initiatives. Mr. Advani has provided consulting services to companies throughout the United States and Latin America and has held interim positions with several of them including CFO and COO. He is a frequent speaker on topics ranging from corporate valuation to financial reporting.

Mr. Advani holds a BA from Yale University, earned an MBA from The Wharton School, and is a university lecturer.